MEAT
PIES

✳

·◦◦◦·

Also by Brian Polcyn and Michael Ruhlman

Pâté, Confit, Rillette: Recipes from the Craft of Charcuterie

Salumi: The Craft of Italian Dry Curing

Charcuterie: The Craft of Salting, Smoking, and Curing

Other Food Books by Michael Ruhlman

The Book of Cocktail Ratios:
The Surprising Simplicity of Classic Cocktails

From Scratch: 10 Meals, 175 Recipes,
and Techniques You'll Use Over and Over

The Making of a Chef: Mastering Heat
at the Culinary Institute of America

The French Laundry Cookbook
(with Thomas Keller and Susie Heller)

The Soul of a Chef: The Journey Toward Perfection

A Return to Cooking (with Eric Ripert)

Bouchon (with Thomas Keller,
Jeffrey Cerciello, and Susie Heller)

The Reach of a Chef: Professional Cooks
in the Age of Celebrity

Under Pressure: Cooking Sous Vide
(with Thomas Keller, Susie Heller, Amy Vogler,
Jonathan Benno, Sebastian Rouxel, and Corey Lee)

The Elements of Cooking: Translating
the Chef's Craft for Every Kitchen

Ratio: The Simple Codes Behind
the Craft of Everyday Cooking

Live to Cook (with Michael Symon)

Ad Hoc at Home (with Thomas Keller,
Dave Cruz, Susie Heller, and Amy Vogler)

Ruhlman's Twenty: 20 Techniques,
100 Recipes, A Cook's Manifesto

Egg: A Culinary Exploration of
the World's Most Versatile Ingredient

Grocery: The Buying and Selling of Food in America

POVR

Hand-Raised Pies (page 67)

Post-Thanksgiving Turkey Pot Pie (page 133)

MEAT
PIES

AN EMERGING
AMERICAN CRAFT

BRIAN POLCYN with
MICHAEL RUHLMAN

Photography by Quentin Bacon

W. W. NORTON & COMPANY
Independent Publishers Since 1923

*For Chefs Milos Cihelka
and Thomas Keller*

Chicken Sheet Pan Pie (page 140)

Contents

Introduction by Michael Ruhlman   11

I. THE BASICS   17
About the Book   18
Tools and Vessels   20
Dough Basics   24
The Three Primary Doughs   28
Gluten-Free Baking   41

II. THE SAVORY PIES   43
Pot Pies   44
Hand-Raised Pies   67
Rolled Raised Pies   83
Tarts and Galettes   103
Double-Crusted Pies   127
Turnovers   153
Vol-au-Vents   165

III. SIDES FOR PIES   179

IV. SAUCES AND CONDIMENTS   187

Acknowledgments   199
Index   203

Cornish-Style Pasties (page 156)

Introduction

by Michael Ruhlman

My personal love of the meat pie began thirty years ago—more than a decade before I teamed up with Brian Polcyn to write our first book together, *Charcuterie*—when I received a letter from my uncle Bill, my father's maternal uncle whose parents hailed from Shropshire, England. Bill was a deeply learned man with a sonorous voice and I, a twenty-eight-year-old aspiring writer. We struck up a lively correspondence between my home in Cleveland and his in Santa Barbara.

His second letter to me began, "Let's see if, at long last, we can get off to you something that might, with some plausibility, be called a letter." And for five single-spaced pages of easy prose, he discoursed on family history, worried over my parents' separation, critiqued my own writing, dismissed the stream-of-consciousness conceit of Joyce, mapped out his own notions of art, discussed the "metaphysics" of Asian cuisine, and offered a remark on a potato he'd eaten years ago during a meal at Galatoire's in New Orleans that would forever guide me in my culinary pursuits.

In a letter a few years later, describing his and his wife Timmie's Christmas morning, he mentioned a pork pie—specifically the pork pie of his mother, a Shropshire lass, Elizabeth Morgan. In my next letter, I asked, "Pork *pie*? What? What is that?" In America, pies are filled with fruit and sugar, not meat.

"For many of the uninitiated," Bill wrote back, "the very notion of pork pie at all (served cold with Colman's mustard)—let alone as a breakfast dish—stirs grimaces of revulsion. But we know of no one who, having come to scoff, hasn't remained to pray."

Pork pie! What an idea it was to me thirty years ago, then a hobby-cook. That a pork pie might be exquisite, that it might be so powerful in its effects as to become a tradition that would stretch from nineteenth-century Shropshire to modern-day Santa Barbara. That it made some want to pray! *This* I had to understand.

I would soon learn in culinary school that the English pork pie was simply a rustic version of the French pâté en croûte, along with all manner of pâtés, typically referred to with the inelegant word *forcemeat* (anglicized from the French verb to stuff, *farcir*). At the time, though, the pork pie merely promised to bring me, in a way that went beyond our letters, closer to Uncle Bill, who had helped me become a writer.

The pork pie is simple: meatloaf in a pie crust. When properly seasoned, though, and gently cooked, it is delicious, with a peppery, garlicky filling and a soft, delectable pastry moistened by the dish's self-contained sauce (we call it aspic here, but to the British it's just jelly). I made my great-grandmother's pork pie, from Bill's elaborate instructions, and knew I had achieved a version worthy of my ancestry when my oldest friend, visiting from his home in London on Christmas Day, swooned as he ate it.

Shropshire is in the center of England, a pork pie hub. One hundred miles east is Melton Mowbray, so well known for meat pies that theirs have geographical protection by law. To the southwest, in the county of Cornwall, wives for centuries have sent their husbands off to the mines with pasties—meat and vegetables within a semicircle of crust and crimped around the edges (the Cornish pasty also has protected geographical status). The crust gave the meat inside a dry protective cover and could be carried in the pocket. An industrious wife might fill one half with pork and the other half with a sweet pudding so that her husband could have lunch with dessert, all in the same crusty package. (If you've seen the movie *Ammonite*, about the nineteenth-century paleontologist Mary Anning, played by Kate Winslet, you may have noticed that the protagonist, scouring the rocky beaches of Lyme, England, pauses in her work to pull a pie from her pocket and eat it for lunch, just as the miners did.)

Australia, colonized by the British as a penal colony in the eighteenth century, has a strong meat pie tradition, as does New Zealand, given their British roots. But then so does the Upper Peninsula of Michigan, which followed the Cornish tradition, baking meat pies for its copper miners. So proud of this tradition are residents of the UP that the village of Calumet, once the center of the state's mining industry, holds an annual Pasty Fest every August.

Only in America are pies sweet. A pie in England is, by definition, filled with meat not fruit, savory not sweet. Fruit pies in Europe are called tarts. America's sweet pies, it's been postulated, came about with the advent of a booming sugar industry in the fruit-rich United States in the nineteenth century, and our subsequent hunger for refined sugar, but everywhere else, from antiquity until today, "pie" meant meat enclosed in a protective paste of flour and water, a substance originally not necessarily meant to be eaten, but one that served as cooking vessel and preservative container, which was sometimes referred to as a coffin.

Some sources date pies to 6000 BCE, about 6,000 years after *Homo sapiens* settled down and began to farm cereal grains and domesticate animals. They were an important part of the cuisine of ancient Rome, and the influence of that empire spread pies globally during the first centuries of the Common Era.

It is possible that the word *pie* derives from the magpie, a bird with a habit of filling its nest with a collection of random items. Pies were a way of combining bits of food and trim and creating an elegant dish out of them. Pies were especially prized in the Middle Ages and were often a source of entertainment at banquets. Game birds were commonly baked into pies—four and twenty black ones, according to the nursery rhyme. And some ancient recipes describe how to fill a pie with small live birds so that they fly out of the pie when it's cut.

By the sixteenth century, all manner of meat—venison, mutton, and game birds—were the stuff of pies, a tradition that would become more and more refined to the point that the English and Australians, by the nineteenth century, were making meat pies worthy of a celebration.

The early settlers of America brought their rich pie tradition with them. There was so much fruit available in the New World that it quickly made it into pies. But savory pies were still the main form of pie until the sugar industry boomed. According to one source, George Washington's favorite pie was a layering of oysters and sweetbreads, bound with a savory custard.

But as the sweet fruit pie proceeded to dominate American culinary culture, the meat pie held fast in Great Britain and remains a grand part of English culture. There, pies are deeply comforting and a part of the national character.

"Something that I've always noticed in restaurants," says Chef Calum Franklin, one of the leading pie experts in England, "it would always be the stressed-out lawyers, the stressed-out journalists who ordered the pies, and I think that for the short period of time of eating it, it takes them back to sitting with Mum, sitting with their brother and sister. It's a bit of comfort eating it. So we have a very strong emotional connection to pies in this country."

⌒

Brian's love of the meat pie came when he was 25, shortly after his mentor, Chef Milos Cihelka, tapped him to take over the Detroit fine-dining restaurant the Lark in the mid-1980s. Meat pies weren't exactly well known here at the time beyond the frozen Swanson supermarket version. But he'd learned a lot under Chef Milos at the famed Golden Mushroom, including pâté en croûte and, by extension, meat pies.

By the time Brian had his own restaurant, he'd developed a relationship with a local farmer who supplied him with beautiful guinea hens, which Brian loves. They're tough birds and best braised. How could he serve these elegantly? In a pot pie, he thought. Perfect. But would it work in a French fine-dining restaurant? It would if he covered the stew of guinea hen, wild mushrooms, and Armagnac in puff pastry. He put it on the menu and that very day, Chef Milos showed up for dinner. Of all the fancy French dishes available, Chef Milos chose the pot pie and raved about it to his friends and, after, to Brian. Brian will never forget how proud he was of that guinea hen pot pie (page 53).

Such refinement has just recently come to the fore in fine dining as food and cooking take on greater prominence throughout the world. Indeed, chefs from as far away as America and Japan descend on Tain l'Hermitage, south of Lyon, France, for the annual Pâté-Croûte World Championships. Chef David Breeden, who leads the kitchen at Thomas Keller's French Laundry in the Napa Valley, has an exceptional pâté en croûte on his Michelin 3-star menu. Angie Mar, then chef of the Beatrice Inn, says she got through the Covid-19 pandemic, in part, thanks to her pies. Pies travel well, so when we were in lockdown, Angie could sell pies to her legions of fans, most notably her bone marrow pie, with a fetching marrow bone sticking out of the crust. (Brian has created his own ode to this pie—see page 61.)

Anthony Rush, a British chef at the Honolulu restaurant Senia, uses vegetable juices to color the lattice doughs that enclose his beef Wellington, one of the most elegant meat pies there is, and one that was duly featured in *Food & Wine*. But turn the page of this same magazine, and there is JP McMahon, a Michelin-starred chef in Galway, Ireland, offering his recipe for Dingle pies, traditional lamb pies from the lush Dingle Peninsula in the southwestern corner of the country.

The aforementioned Calum Franklin, formerly executive chef of Holborn Dining Room in London, became one of the leaders in this pie renaissance when he opened the Pie Room within the restaurant. It started innocently: He came across a mold, a "corset mold" he would later learn, and had no idea what it was. He asked his fellow chefs if they knew. No one did and so he began looking into it. He became fascinated with pies and soon began wowing the world on Instagram with his extraordinary pies featuring elaborate decorative dough work.

Meat pies, many thousands of years old, are new again. These chefs and others helped spark a renewed love of and fascination with cooking around the globe that, in the United States, truly began to blossom thanks to the work of James Beard and Julia Child in the 1960s. Today cooks and eaters are ready to embrace meat pies—indeed, all kinds of savory pies—as never before.

Brian and I have been among them as we explored pâté en croûte in our book *Charcuterie*, and then again in *Pâté, Confit, Rillette*. We have worked together for years as teachers, writers, and cooks to educate both professional chefs and home cooks. Our books are teaching books, since cooking is fundamentally a craft and all crafts can be taught. Brian has been a teacher of charcuterie at Schoolcraft College outside Detroit for 27 years. One section of his class covers meat cooked in crust, whether for a meat pie or for a show-stopping pâté en croûte. And this has been one of the great benefits of his work at Schoolcraft: He *teaches* the recipes he's created for this book, so they have been tested over and over by his culinary students.

All of our books have focused on utility, on how to create extraordinary dishes by taking advantage of underused and lesser-known cuts of meat and using trim from cooking the expensive cuts. This ability to use every morsel of food to create dishes that are more than the sum of their parts in many ways defines the chef. The meat pie is the perfect example. Born of utility and practicality, it almost always uses less desirable and less expensive cuts of meat—this alone, using off-cuts of meat, and using less of them, is part of the modern mandate of reducing our meat consumption for our own health and the health of the environment. Pies are good for the planet!

Another aspect of the meat pie's utility is that it provides a means of using leftovers to create beautiful new meals. After a great roast chicken dinner, a basic chicken pot pie becomes a second, deeply satisfying meal, if you save the leftover meat and simmer the carcass in the oven to make an easy stock (page 189). Leftover pot roast can likewise be transformed into a glorious pie (page 149). Even the ends and trim from salmon, or from virtually any fish, can be turned into a pie with a little know-how (page 60).

Brian and I are eager to bring both poetry and practicality, as well as recipes and compelling photographs (thank you, Quentin Bacon), to the great variety of savory pies in our culinary world—not just meat pies, but also vegetable pies, cheese pies, seafood pies, and almost-pies (such as a potato-topped seafood pie). This book will delve into the savory pie in order to perfect all its components, the many possible crusts, the infinite fillings, and the accompanying sauces.

When we explore the fundamentals of the craft, we reveal the power these fundamentals give to a cook. Fundamentals are a cook's muscles, and they are the path to true creativity. Our greatest hope is that we convey to you the fundamentals of this ancient craft so that together we can move the craft forward.

—

How miraculously food connects us. Had Elizabeth Morgan not made a pork pie every Christmas in Shropshire, England, her son might not have continued to make it late into the twentieth century, and therefore I might never have had that connection, through food, to this man who scarcely knew how important he was to me.

Bill's instructions for pork pie were so elaborate they might have scared off a less intrepid home cook than I—molding dough around a 6-inch-wide container to create the shell and leaving it in a cold foyer overnight, simmering a stock of pork bones to make the jelly, and so on. Much of this labor, I would eventually figure out, was unnecessary—just hurdles born of the Brits' eccentric culinary heritage (and former lack of refrigeration).

But the two pages of typed instructions—which began with "Two or three days ahead, boil the bones" and concluded with "On the 25th, it is pork pie time (breakfast at our house after Bloody Marys)"—in Bill's letter weren't enough to satisfy him. Bill penned a two-page postscript, with diagrams, addressing the thickness of the crust and other matters of finesse he felt, on rereading, the recipe lacked. Bill concluded with his customary eloquence and generosity: "But here I go, saying both too much and too little. In the end it's a matter between you and the cooking gods. May they smile on you."

Uncle Bill died of a stroke in 1999. Would that I had time enough for one last letter to say the words I never did: "Dear Bill, they have. Thanks for everything. Not least, the pork pie. Maybe we can write a book about it one day."

One among many folds to make a flaky
Blitz Puff Pastry Dough (page 36)

I

✳

THE
BASICS

About the Book   18

Tools and Vessels   20

Dough Basics   24

The Three Primary Doughs   29

  3-2-1 Pie Dough   33

  Pâte Brisée   33

  Blitz Puff Pastry Dough 36

Gluten-Free Baking   41

ABOUT
THE BOOK

In this book we intend to help you not only perfect the meat pie but also broaden the range of pies available to you. While some pies, like the pot pie (a stew topped with a crust), are dead simple, all pies are not. This book aims to teach you all about pies so that you don't make mistakes and so that you can minimize the challenges you may face when you enclose something savory and delicious in a rich crust. The world of pies is vast, and here we cover the fundamental types of pies of the Western culinary canon. Pies appear throughout the world, but this book does not intend to be an international survey of pies, interesting though these pies may be. The pies in this book include the main forms of the meat pie, from individual, hand-raised pies, to rolled, raised pies, to turnovers and vol-au-vents; meat pies, fish pies, vegetable pies, and cheese pies.

Of course, the vehicle that makes any admixture of ingredients a pie is the crust. We don't have pie if we don't have a crust. And so we spend a good amount of time discussing crusts, what makes them good (rich, flaky, crunchy) or bad (tough and chewy), the different kinds of crusts, and why we use one crust rather than another in any given preparation.

While we describe numerous crusts, most of these recipes use one of three fundamental doughs: the versatile 3-2-1 pie dough, the rich pâte brisée, and a blitz puff pastry dough that has some rise to it. We'll discuss all dough basics, how they work, what makes them good or not (for instance, all doughs benefit from a good rest in the fridge before rolling them out, and a tiny amount of vinegar prevents oxidation during this rest). We also love our biscuit dough and sour cream dough, and Brian has developed his own gluten-free dough.

Because the crust is what makes a pie, we've divided the book into sections defined by the crust. We begin with the contemporary pot pie, and move on to hand-raised pies (individual pies), rolled-raised pies, double-crusted pies, turnovers, and a chapter on vol-au-vents (flaky little filled pastry shells).

We also describe the equipment that is most valuable to us and that we believe will be most valuable to you in your kitchen. For a basic meat pie, you need only a knife, a pair of hands, and an oven, but for more elaborate pies and decorative pies, a few vessels and tools come in handy.

Most pies are complete and satisfying meals when served with a simple salad or a side of mashed potatoes, and to that end we offer a few recipe suggestions for what to serve with pies. We also have a range of sauces, gravies, and condiments that enhance the pie eating experience, and we conclude *Meat Pies* with these.

⁓

One of the most important features of this book are its step-by-step photographs, which will help you visualize what your dough and your pies should look like at each stage of their making.

We think it's important to reiterate how the recipes in this book were developed and tested. It has been Brian's great good fortune to be a teacher of the charcuterie course for more than a quarter century at Schoolcraft College in suburban Detroit (in addition to creating some of the area's finest restaurants). One of the specialties of the charcutier is the pie. Brian *teaches* the pie. He creates the various pie recipes. And these recipes are given to the students to learn from. A side benefit to this teaching is that with each new rotation of culinary students, we have a new batch of recipe testers. These are recipes that have been made not just once, but over and over.

It's been a reassuring pleasure to talk to people about pies. Every time someone asked us what we were working on, and we said, "meat pies," that person all but invariably said, "Oh, I *love* meat pies." So do we. And if you're reading this, so do you. Welcome to our world of pies!

⁓

An Important Note About Salt

There are so many salts available today, it's no wonder many people are confused. Himalayan pink salt, black salt, sel gris, fleur de sel, Maldon salt—these salts are fundamentally about texture and, to a lesser degree, minerality. We don't recommend using any of them for cooking. We recommend using coarse kosher salt exclusively for cooking.

Two brands dominate the market: Diamond Crystal and Morton's. Diamond Crystal has long been the mainstay in restaurant kitchens, while Morton's has been the choice at home. Recently, though, Diamond Crystal has moved into the supermarket aisle, so both are now widely available.

But they are not identical. Their shape differs: A grain of Morton's kosher salt is more like a cube, whereas a grain of Diamond Crystal is more of a flake. This means that they fill a measuring spoon differently. Morton's is "saltier"—a tablespoon of Morton's salt is more powerful than a tablespoon of Diamond Crystal. (Chef Jean-Georges Vongerichten, a Diamond Crystal user, once found himself working in a kitchen that used Morton's, and he couldn't figure out why all his dishes were coming out so salty.)

Is one better than the other? Some chefs claim that Diamond Crystal has a purer flavor since Morton's contains an anti-caking agent. But we don't think that really matters; it's still salt. Here is what is important: Choose one and use that one exclusively. Over time you will have an intuitive sense of how much salt you're adding by touch.

All the recipes in this book were developed and tested using Diamond Crystal. If you use Morton's kosher salt and are measuring by volume (that is, using a measuring spoon), reduce the amount of salt called for in these recipes by approximately 25 percent. Sometimes it's an easy conversion (4 teaspoons of Diamond Crystal equals roughly 3 teaspoons of Morton's). But if it's not, use your eye and common sense to reduce the amount.

If you are measuring by weight—which we recommend, especially when making dough—the two are interchangeable: 12 grams of Diamond Crystal has the same effect as 12 grams of Morton's.

TOOLS AND VESSELS

Your kitchen probably already has everything you need to make a basic pie—your hands, a knife, a bowl, measuring cups, an oven—but there are some additional items that make the work both easier and more satisfying.

① **Rolling pin:** We recommend a big, solid, heavy rolling pin over a French rolling pin (the kind that is slightly tapered at either end), since the best way to roll out dough is to let the weight of the pin do the rolling rather than leaning hard on the pin as you roll, which can create an uneven dough, which then tends to proceed into an irregular shape. Ultimately, though, this is a matter of preference.

② **Pans:** Some pies require no cooking vessel at all, but most do. For this book, we use a 10 by 1-inch/25 by 2.5-centimeter fluted tart pan with a removable bottom and a 9-inch/23-centimeter pie plate. All the recipes in this book have been scaled for these sizes.

③ **Pie dolly:** This is a wooden cylinder about 3 inches/7.5 centimeters in diameter and 6 inches/15 centimeters tall, including the handle, used for shaping individual hand-raised pies. One presses the dolly into a disk of dough and raises the dough up around it with one's fingers. We love the simplicity of design; it's pleasing as a kitchen object alone. A rule of thumb for these single-portion pies is you will need a 6-ounce/170-gram piece of dough for the bottom and a 2-ounce/60-gram piece of dough for the top.

Digital scale: This isn't strictly required for pies, but it certainly makes measuring flour and fat easier. It's the most accurate way to measure flour, arguably the most important ingredient in pies as, without it, you don't really have a pie. A cup or two of flour can vary in weight by as much as 50 percent. If you do a lot of baking, a digital scale is a relatively inexpensive but invaluable tool.

Pot pie dishes: Ceramic, earthenware, or enameled cast-iron individual pie dishes are great to have on hand to turn leftovers into an elegant single-crusted pot pie. We prefer straight-sided dishes that hold 2 cups/480 milliliters; they should have a handle, as pot pies tend to bubble over and a handle makes moving them easy. Apply an egg wash to the bottom of the dough so that it seals along the rim.

④ **Rimmed baking sheets/sheet pans:** Skip those flimsy, inexpensive baking sheets in favor of heavy-duty pans that transfer heat well and don't buckle over time. We recommend standard half sheet pans, which are 18 by 13 inches/46 by 33 centimeters.

⑤ **Pastry brushes:** These are a must for applying egg wash, and quality matters here. It's the same philosophy as buying a paintbrush at the hardware store: You can buy a $1 brush or you can buy a $10 brush, and they're priced differently for a reason. Look for natural bristles, the finer the better. We don't recommend using silicone brushes, which carry too much egg wash, and the thick "bristles" make it difficult to achieve a uniform coat.

⑥ **Lattice cutter:** This is an optional tool, but it's great if you make a lot of pies. It consists of numerous circular, interrupted blades that cut offset dashes in a piece of dough, allowing you to spread the dough into a wide lattice (see page 131). It makes for a beautiful top to all manner of pies. When making a lattice top, be sure the dough is very cold when cutting. And it's a good idea to go over the cuts with a paring knife to ensure it all spreads out evenly, as sometimes the blade doesn't go all the way through. This typically happens when one of the blades, getting knocked around in a drawer or tool kit, gets dinged. So it's a good idea to keep it wrapped in a towel if it's stored with other tools.

Docker: A pie docker, a series of pins protruding from a cylinder (imagine a paint roller with pins sticking out), is convenient if you're docking (pricking) a lot of pies or large pies that are

prebaked (blind baked) to prevent the bottom from puffing up irregularly from steam during the baking, but it's not critical. The tines are small and this is important: If the holes are too big, liquidy fillings can leak through the baked crust. So when using a fork, keep in mind that you want to make holes as little as possible. And always dock the dough when it's raw rather than partially baked.

⑦ **Dough crimper:** A dough crimper seals the dough while creating a decorative pattern.

⑧ **Pie weights:** Pie weights prevent the dough from puffing up irregularly from steam during blind baking (baking an empty shell). If you're making a lot of pies, heatproof marble-shaped weights can be useful and are reusable. We use dried beans, which work just as well (you can reuse the beans as pie weights, but not for cooking). We only blind bake single-crusted pies with wet fillings.

⑨ ⑩ **Pastry blender and bench scraper:** Both of these tools are also known as dough cutters. We often work on a marble surface, which would quickly dull a knife, so we use these tools to cut the dough instead. You can also cut butter into a dough with them. And of course the bench scraper is a good tool for scraping up dough and flour from your work surface. We prefer a metal bench scraper with a wooden handle. We especially like to use one engraved with inch and centimeter marks so that it doubles as a measuring device.

Box grater: For most of his career, Brian has diced butter using a knife and plenty of flour to keep the butter from sticking when preparing butter to add to flour for a dough. During the writing of this book, he discovered that grating very cold butter on the large holes of a box grater directly into the flour is faster, easier, and neater.

⑪ **Parchment paper:** We find that we get better browning on the bottom of our doughs when we line our sheet pans with parchment paper rather than silicone baking mats, but those will do for convenience.

Meat grinder: Meat pies often use some form of ground meat. Hobart is the king of grinders in professional kitchens, but a small electric meat grinder is best for the home and is critical for making excellent sausage. For these pies, though, we can also recommend the grinder attachment for your standing mixer. Just remember to keep whatever meat and fat you intend to grind very, very cold.

Standing mixer: A standing mixer is useful for mixing dough (and, with an attachment, for grinding meat). Just take care not to overmix the dough. Using a paddle attachment, mix the dough just until it comes together.

Digital thermometer: This is a great tool to have in the kitchen for measuring the internal temperature of dishes, especially important when making larger pies that require longer cooking. We like a thermometer that has a probe that folds, so that you can measure with the probe out straight or at 90 degrees. Cable thermometers that remain in the meat or pâté throughout the cooking are convenient too, allowing you to monitor the temperature without opening the oven. Some of them connect wirelessly to your smartphone to alert you when a preset temperature is reached.

⑫ **Round cutters:** We recommend both fluted and straight cutters, in a variety of sizes, which are handy for achieving consistent sizes when cutting out dough.

⑬ **Small offset spatula:** We use this inexpensive tool for pressing ground meat into the corners of a dough-lined pan. They're also good tools generally for lifting small items.

Ruler: A good, sturdy ruler with a clean, straight edge is useful in the kitchen for measuring dough and using as a cutting jig for long, straight cuts. Brian uses a yardstick at school, but a 12-inch/30-centimeter wooden or metal ruler is fine at home.

⑭ **Scissors:** Buy sturdy kitchen scissors for multiple uses in the kitchen. We prefer scissors with pointed blades for cleaner snips when cutting decorative steam vents.

Fine-mesh sieve: This is a useful tool to have on hand for general straining. Here we recommend it for straining egg yolks to remove the chalazae when making large batches of egg wash (see page 28).

Knives: When it comes to knives, sharpness is more important than quality. One of the biggest faults in home kitchens and one of the biggest obstacles in cooking in general is a dull knife. As Brian says, a sharp $12 knife is better than a dull $400 knife. Get your knives professionally sharpened, learn to sharpen them yourself, or buy new inexpensive knives regularly. Three good, sharp knives are critical in the kitchen: a small paring knife, an 8-inch/20-centimeter chef's knife or other larger knife, and a serrated bread knife for cutting crusts and bread.

A good pastry brush is important for a smooth, uniform coating of egg wash. This is the Mediterranean Vegetable Pie. See page 88 for the result.

DOUGH BASICS

Flour, Fat, Water: How It All Comes Together

Dough is a mixture of flour and fat, to which a little water is added, bringing the fat and flour together as one. Flour contains the protein gluten, which, as you work a dough, forms long elastic strands. These become, with enough mixing, delightfully chewy. This is why we knead bread dough for so long, and knead pasta dough until it's smooth and supple. But we don't want a pie dough to be chewy; we want it to be tender and flaky. The fat, whether butter, shortening, or lard, gets in between those strands, preventing them from linking up, shortening them. Which is why these doughs are often called short doughs.

A short dough should have a tender, flaky, crumbly crust, one that is rich and flavorful thanks to the fat. This fat can be sweet, in the form of butter, or savory, in the form of lard.

The fat matters in two ways. First, flavor. Lard, especially lard you render yourself, can have a distinct porky flavor and aroma, which is fabulous for pork pies but even for well-spiced apple pies and other fruits that go well with pork. It's more than worth the effort. When rendering pork fat for doughs, be sure to render it so that it stays as pale as possible. If it gets too hot it will brown and take on roasted flavors, which will overpower the dough. And if you can find leaf lard, lard that comes from the interior of the pig, surrounding the kidneys, render this to make the finest pastry fat.

Butter, of course, is the fat of choice as it's always on hand. Our preference is for unsalted butter, but salted is fine as well, if you omit the salt in the recipe or learn from experience whether salt is required for the dough. Importantly, butter includes water, about 15 percent of its weight, along with solids that brown flavorfully at higher temperatures. This means you need slightly more water when using lard than when using butter.

As a rule, the fat and flour are mixed together until the mixture becomes mealy, either by hand, dough cutter, or standing mixer with the paddle attachment. Larger chunks of butter—some recipes call for pea-size chunks of butter—can create holes in the dough, which is undesirable. Except for the Blitz Puff Pastry Dough (page 36), we prefer our fat uniformly mixed. Again, using the large holes of a box grater, grating the butter directly into the flour, is our preferred way to cut butter into a dough.

Mixing warms the butter, something you must be aware of. This is why we add ice-cold water to the dough once the fat is mixed in. As soon as the water is added, the gluten will begin linking up. The less this happens, the more flaky the dough. So it's important to work the dough, by hand, only just until it comes together en masse. Working the dough too much will toughen it.

Once you've achieved a smooth, uniform dough, stop. Form the dough into one or more 1-inch/2.5-centimeter-thick pieces, circular or rectangular, depending on what the finished dish is. Wrap it in plastic and refrigerate it for at least 20 minutes; we believe that dough is at its peak after a 24-hour refrigeration.

On Rolling

First, as you are always working on a floured surface, be aware that your dough will pick up the flour on your board. So use only enough to keep the dough from sticking to the board. If it sticks, it won't roll out evenly. Flick the flour sideways, parallel to the board so you get an even spread, rather than sprinkling from on high as you would season a steak with salt.

Second, always roll away from you, not back toward yourself, which can result in an uneven dough. If you are simply too used to rolling back and forth, do not put any pressure on the back roll. It's all about maintaining an even thickness, and not developing imperceptible waves in your dough from uneven pressure when rolling. Even when rolling forward, don't press down too hard on the rolling pin; press only gently, letting the weight of the pin do the spreading.

Rather than roll all the way past the edge of the dough, stop just at the edge so that the edges will be the same thickness as the rest of the dough—if you go over the edge, the edge will be tapered.

Turn your dough, not your body. After rolling, rotate the dough 90 degrees and roll, turn and roll. And take your time. Take a long time. The single fact you must acknowledge and obey when working with virtually any dough, whether pie dough or bread dough, is that dough cannot be rushed. If you try to roll it too fast, you will see an elastic retreat by the dough. Let it rest. Popping it back in the fridge is never a bad idea. Indeed, temperature is very important. If your kitchen is very hot, it's important to chill the dough if you sense that it's getting too warm and soft.

If you're making a rectangular dough, once your dough has softened somewhat and has been rolled out halfway, you can go in two directions. Begin in the center and roll out toward one corner, then the other. Turn the dough 180 degrees and repeat.

Again, take your time. Making dough should be a sensory pleasure, in terms of both sight and texture. It's lovely to see and touch.

When you've finished rolling—check to make sure you've rolled it out big enough, allowing for bottom, sides, and an inch of overhang—line your pan. Tart pans and pie dishes virtually line themselves: Fold the dough in half and then in half again, place the folded corner in the center of the pan, and unfold it. Once you have the dough in the pan, use the back of your finger to press the dough into the bottom edge to make sure there are no air pockets. Or take a scrap of excess dough, shape it into a ball, and use this ball to press the dough into the edges. Then gradually work out the folds, pressing the dough firmly against the sides of the pan.

Refrigerate your dough for at least an hour once you've lined your pan. This is critical, as the butter within the dough must be completely solid. Chilling the dough will help it maintain its shape when it goes into the oven; if you neglect to thoroughly chill it, the dough may shrink too much and develop cracks. Chilling is especially important when blind baking a crust.

On Blind Baking

Blind baking means prebaking a tart or pie crust before filling it. This is especially important when you are filling it with a custard or anything wet. We never blind bake a crust for a pie that will be topped by dough.

Many of the recipes in this book call for blind baking a tart shell using a pâte brisée or 3-2-1 pie dough. When blind baking rich doughs, leave a 2-inch/5-centimeter overhang because doughs that are higher in fat tend to shrink most during the baking. The excess is easily trimmed after the pie is done.

How to Blind Bake

1. Preheat the oven to 350°F/175°C.

2. Roll out the dough to the desired thickness and line your tart mold or pie plate with the dough. Dock the dough with a fork. Place a sheet of aluminum foil or parchment paper over the dough, then fill with dried beans or pie weights. Bake for 20 minutes, then remove the foil and weights and bake for another 10 to 15 minutes to finish cooking and browning the dough.

3. Remove from the oven and allow to cool completely before filling.

On Moisture Barriers

Some meat pies and most pâtés en croûte call for lining the crust with a layer of thinly sliced bacon, ham, or fat (caul fat or pork back fat). Moist fillings that are wrapped in dough, particularly with rolled raised pies, often require some sort of barrier to prevent moisture and juices from saturating the dough and making it soggy. A moisture barrier can add flavor and richness, but it doesn't typically contribute a lot of flavor to a finished dish.

Cooked crepes ready to be used as a
moisture barrier.

We've found that fish is too moist even when it's finished cooking and releases enough moisture to make the bottom soggy and steam the rest. So we typically make very thin crêpes and line our dough with these to ensure a crisp finished crust when enclosing fish in dough. Lining your dough with crêpes allows you to achieve a crispy crust because the protein from the egg keeps the moisture in. Crêpes are very quick and easy to make, especially if you have a good nonstick skillet (or a crêpe pan, of course). This recipe will also work if you simply want to have crêpes for breakfast. Just omit the parsley and add a couple teaspoons of sugar and a dash of vanilla.

Crêpes

2   large eggs
⅓   cup/80 milliliters whole milk
2   tablespoons chopped fresh flat-leaf
       parsley
       Kosher salt and freshly ground black
       pepper to taste
½   cup/60 grams all-purpose flour
       Vegetable oil or clarified butter,
       for frying

1. In a medium bowl, whisk the eggs, milk, parsley, salt, and pepper until smooth. While whisking, sprinkle or sift in the flour until it's smoothly incorporated.

2. Heat an 8-inch/20-centimeter nonstick skillet over medium heat. Add just enough oil or butter to coat the bottom. Holding the pan in the air, ladle in just enough batter to coat the bottom, tilting and rolling the pan to make a thin crêpe. Cook just until set, about 1 minute, then transfer to a plate. Repeat to make the remaining crêpes.

MAKES 4 OR 5 CRÊPES

Filling Basics

Air pockets are evil and the enemy of pies as they can wreck a crust when slicing if the crispy dough has no inner support. So be sure when filling your pans that there are no air pockets. Always push the filling down into the corners.

The Vent Hole

Most covered pies should be vented to allow steam to escape in a controlled way. We typically either make decorative snips or cut circular vent holes in the lid. This allows the meat to cook and the crust to become crisp.

For many meat pies, the filling will bubble up through the vent hole and run out onto the crust. This can be appealingly rustic and homey. But for pies that must be beautiful, it's not enough to simply cut a hole. You should also fashion a chimney out of aluminum foil and surround it with a small piece of dough. This allows steam to escape, but any bubbling liquids will not overflow the vent hole and discolor your beautiful pie. We employ a foil chimney in the recipes for American Pekin Duck Pie with Pistachios (page 134) and, pictured below, Chicken Sheet Pan Pie (page 140).

Egg Wash

Egg washing contributes to the dough's finish and makes a pie look glossy and golden brown. Some egg washes use a whole egg with water and others use only the yolk with water. After years of egg washing pies, we don't see any reason to use anything other than the yolk-only egg wash below. We love the deep brown hue it gives a pie.

In professional kitchens that use a lot of egg wash, the yolks will be passed through a fine-mesh sieve to ensure that the chalazae are removed. Chalazae are the white protein bundles attached to either pole of the yolk that keep the yolk suspended in the center of the egg when in its shell. These can mar an otherwise smooth and uniform egg wash and even burn in the oven. So while it's not essential that you pass your egg wash through a sieve when using just a couple of yolks, it is essential to remove the chalazae from the yolk before mixing it with the water.

Egg Wash

2   large egg yolks
     Pinch kosher salt
1   tablespoon water

Put the yolks in a small bowl and, using your fingers, remove the chalazae. (If you're making larger quantities of egg wash, we recommend passing the yolks through a sieve to remove the chalazae.) Add the salt, then whisk in the water.

Note: Perhaps the most important thing to avoid when egg washing a pie are pools of egg wash. Use egg wash sparingly and apply it as evenly as you would paint a wall. Egg wash is best when applied in two coats. It's one of the most important steps in creating a delicious-looking pie and is worth the time. Give the pie one coat of egg wash. Refrigerate it for 15 minutes or longer, then give it a second coat.

On Decorating Dough

Almost always you will have scraps of dough left after cutting your crust or crusts. These scraps can be rolled out and used to embellish your pie. Double-crusted pies and larger sheet pan pies will look appealing with simple decorations such as vines, leaves, and flowers. For pot pies, maybe something more dramatic, such as antlers for a venison pie (page 64) or guinea fowl for a guinea fowl pie (page 53).

Leaves and vines can be cut freehand. For the more elaborate decorations, search the internet for images, which Brian did, for example, with the antlers. Size the image on a computer, print it, and cut out a stencil. Put the stencil on the rolled-out dough and trace it with your paring knife.

For a successful decoration, use this method:

First, egg wash the undecorated top of your pie and chill the pie for 15 minutes or so. When it's chilled, egg wash your decorative pieces. Then give your pie a second egg wash. Before this egg wash dries, place the decorative pieces on the top using a small offset spatula or knife. Re-chill the pie for about 15 minutes, until the egg wash is set.

And that's all there is too it!

The Three Primary Doughs

Our go-to dough for most pies is the versatile 3-2-1 Pie Dough (page 33), so named because that is its recipe: 3 parts flour, 2 parts butter (or lard), 1 part water. It's easy to make. It's easy to work with. Most importantly, it's delicious (it's one-third butter, after all). If you use only one dough, this would be it. Every pie in this book can be made with this dough.

Because it's less fatty than pâte brisée, the 3-2-1 pie dough tends to have more structure and hold up better in cooking, especially for something like a pâté en croûte, but it's still satisfyingly rich. Hold back on the water when making it, adding just enough to bring the dough together so it remains tender. Butter is roughly 15 percent water, so you need less water than you would if you were using only lard.

Pâte Brisée (page 33) is higher in fat, with equal parts flour and butter. Because it's so rich, it's best used in some kind of mold. When we make a tart in a tart pan, this is the dough we choose.

As a rule, 3-2-1 Pie Dough and Pâte Brisée doughs are best if they've rested overnight in the fridge. It's not essential, of course; you can make a perfectly fine pie with dough you mixed 10 minutes ago. But for the best workability and texture, overnight is best.

Blitz Puff Pastry Dough (page 36) mimics traditional puff pastry in the way it's brought together and rolled out. Traditional puff pastry is made by enclosing a block of butter in a standard dough, rolling it out, then folding it in thirds like a letter and rolling it out again. These folds and rolls are repeated multiple times to create what's called a laminated dough, with hundreds of layers of butter between twice as many layers of dough. It puffs when it bakes. Add yeast and you have the dough used for croissants.

Our blitz puff pastry uses a technique that mimics the layering of traditional puff pastry. Fraisage calls for flattening chunks of butter into thin sheets using a rolling pin, rather than paddling the flour and butter in a standing mixer until the flour resembles coarse meal. Cream is then used as the liquid to bring the dough together. Given the fat content of cream, this dough is almost equal parts fat and flour, like pâte brisée.

When making puff pastry, it's important to start with cold flour and keep the dough very cold or the butter can become too soft. If that happens, distinct layers won't form and you will have no puff. It should have at least two hour-long rests in the fridge between folds.

Puff pastry is the perfect dough for pot pies, which traditionally get a layer of puff. Its light, airy texture and rich flavor are the perfect match for the chicken, beef, or game stew beneath it.

Miscellaneous Doughs

In addition to the three basic doughs for most of our pies, there are a few outliers we like. We use a hot water dough for individual, hand-raised pies. We love how quickly and easily it comes together and how workable the dough is. It has a lovely crisp finish when baked. But

it can be tricky to work with—it's very hot when first mixed, but it's important to shape the dough when it's not too hot and not too cool.

We also realize that many people, for various reasons, avoid gluten, so Brian has developed a gluten-free dough. He swears by the mixture created by Cup4Cup for ease and convenience. This dough can be used for any and all pies for those avoiding gluten.

We use a biscuit crust for the Chicken Pot Pie (page 48), a great technique for any pot pie if you love biscuits. The recipe for an excellent dough enriched with sour cream is used with the German Heirloom Cottage Cheese Pie (page 105). This dough is softer than traditional dough and won't get crispy. It's best suited for savory or sweet brunch-style pies featuring cottage cheese, ricotta cheese, or farmers cheese.

An Important Note about Dough Yields

The following doughs result in differing yields because the proportions given in the recipe work best. Some recipes will make more dough than you will need. Fortunately, thanks to their high fat content, doughs freeze well. Indeed, if pies are a regular part of your cooking routine, we recommend making big batches of dough and freezing them in 12-ounce/340-gram and 1½-pound/680-gram portions. Well wrapped, they will stay fresh for a month or two so that they're ready to thaw and roll out whenever you want to throw together a pie.

If you want to make just enough dough for one pie, use the 3-2-1 Pie Dough recipe. One recipe will be enough for a double-crusted pie; halve the recipe for just enough dough for one tart shell.

The Crimping Process

① Egg wash the rim of dough in the tart pan, put the dough lid on, and seal it tightly.

② Pinch the dough so that it extends beyond the rim of the pie.

③ Fold the dough back over onto itself to create a bead, or thick rim, ready for crimping.

④ Use a three-finger crimp to make a decorative edge by pressing an index finger into the inner side of the rim, while pressing the thumb and index finger of your other hand into the outer side of the rim.

⑤ Work your way around the entire rim.

Spinach and Mushroom
Galette (page 116), using the
Pâte Brisée dough (page 33)

3-2-1 Pie Dough

12 ounces/340 grams all-purpose flour
(about 2½ cups)
½ teaspoon/3 grams kosher salt
8 ounces/225 grams unsalted butter (or half
unsalted butter and half lard), chilled
½ cup/120 milliliters ice water
¼ teaspoon distilled white vinegar
(optional; see Note)

1. Combine the flour and salt in a large bowl.
Using the large holes on a box grater, grate the
butter (and lard, if using) into the bowl. (You
can also small-dice the butter using a knife
and add it to the flour.) Mix the butter and flour
together with your hands until the mixture
resembles coarse meal; it should not become too
warm or pasty.

2. Add the water and vinegar (if using) and mix
until a dough forms.

3. Divide the dough in half, wrap in plastic
wrap, and refrigerate for at least 1 hour and up
to 24 hours.

4. Let the dough temper at room temperature for
30 minutes before rolling.

YIELD: 1½ POUNDS/680 GRAMS DOUGH (enough
for one double-crusted pie; halve the recipe for a
single-crusted pie or tart shell)

> *Note:* Although you can roll out this dough
> after chilling for 1 hour, it will still be very
> elastic. It's best to let this dough chill for at
> least 6 hours before rolling. Some feel it's
> best kept overnight. If you are going to make
> your dough a day ahead, as we recommend,
> do add the optional vinegar as it helps
> preserve the dough and prevent oxidation.

Pâte Brisée

1 pound/450 grams all-purpose flour
(about 3¼ cups)
1 tablespoon/12 grams kosher salt
1 pound/450 grams unsalted butter, chilled
1 large egg
Water, as needed

1. Combine the flour and salt in a large bowl.
Using the large holes on a box grater, grate the
butter into the bowl. (You can also small-dice
the butter using a knife and add it to the flour.)
Cut the butter into the flour and salt. Rub the
mixture between your fingers until it resembles
coarse meal.

2. Crack the egg into a liquid measuring cup. Add
enough water so that the total volume equals 1
cup/240 milliliters, then whisk with a fork until
uniformly blended. Add the egg and water to
the flour-butter mixture and mix by hand into a
uniform paste.

3. Wrap the dough in plastic and chill for at least
1 hour. Let the dough temper at room temperature for 30 minutes before rolling.

YIELD: 2½ POUNDS/1.15 KILOGRAMS DOUGH

3-2-1 Dough and Pâte Brisée Process

① While writing this book, Brian chanced upon this excellent method for cutting butter into dough: grating it directly into the flour. Though dicing butter works as it always has, it takes more effort than grating, as you have to flour the butter to keep it from sticking.

② Grating the butter is faster and the resulting long curls are easily kneaded into the flour to create a shaggy mixture. Dough instructions often call for the texture to be like coarse meal, but we like the butter to be in larger chunks so that the butter spreads in thin layers and gives the finished dough a fluffier, flakier texture.

③ Water is what transforms the flour-butter mixture into dough, as it allows the gluten molecules to link up and binds the flour particles. It's important to use ice water to keep the butter firm.

④ The dough comes together quickly by hand. Mix only until it coalesces into a ball. Overmixing can result in a tough crust.

❺ The finished dough—3 parts flour, 2 parts butter, 1 part water—is ready to be shaped into a disk, wrapped in plastic, and refrigerated until chilled.

Blitz Puff Pastry Dough

- 1 pound/450 grams all-purpose flour (about 3¼ cups), chilled, plus more for dusting
- 8 ounces/225 grams unsalted butter, chilled and cut into 1-tablespoon pieces
- 1 tablespoon/12 grams kosher salt
- 2 cups/480 milliliters heavy cream, chilled

1. Put the cold flour on a work surface. Sprinkle the butter pats into it and coat evenly with flour. Use a rolling pin and the fraisage method (see page 29 and page 38, photo 2) to flatten the butter into the flour, leaving thin sheets of butter.

2. In a small bowl, dissolve the salt into the cream. Add the cream to the flour mixture in three separate stages, incorporating the cream each time with a plastic bench scraper. After the last addition of cream, the mass should slightly resemble a shaggy paste. Flatten this mass into a rectangle as best as you can.

3. Very lightly dust the dough with flour and roll it into a rectangle, ¼ inch/6 millimeters thick and three times as long as it is wide. Fold the dough in thirds as you would a letter, rotate the dough 90 degrees, then roll out the dough again into the same dimensions. Repeat the folding and rolling one more time, then fold it in thirds again, wrap it in plastic, and refrigerate it for 1 hour (to prevent the butter from getting too soft).

4. Remove the dough from the fridge and repeat the rolling and folding two more times. Then fold it in thirds, rewrap it, and refrigerate it for another hour or, better, overnight.

YIELD: 2 POUNDS/900 GRAMS DOUGH

① The first step in making **Blitz Puff Pastry Dough** is to toss the chunks of butter with the chilled flour so that they don't stick to each other. This dough is temperature sensitive, so it's important that all your ingredients, including the flour, have been refrigerated and that you bring this dough together quickly. (This is not the time to answer your phone or check your Instagram feed!) This is also a messy, raggedy dough. Don't attempt to make this dough on a notebook-size cutting board. If you don't have a large cutting board, clear a space on your counter and work directly on that.

② With a heavy rolling pin, roll the butter into the flour, flattening the chunks into sheets.

③ This is messy, but it will come together. Have faith in the flour. You're adding the cream in three different stages. It's important to have a bench scraper on hand to catch the cream.

④ Continue adding the cream and using the bench scraper to fold the flour from the edges into the center until all the cream has been absorbed.

⑤ When the cream has been absorbed, you'll be able to shape the dough into a rectangle. It will still be loose and shaggy.

⑥ Once you've shaped the rectangle, make your first fold. You may need to scrape it off your board with the bench scraper.

⑦ After you've folded the final third of the dough over on itself (you're folding this the way you would fold a letter to put in an envelope), turn the dough 90 degrees so that the narrow edge is facing you.

⑧ Roll out the folded dough. You should be able to see the thin sheets of butter within the dough.

⑨ Repeat the folds using the letter method. Turn the dough 90 degrees and roll it out again. This is your second of four turns.

Blitz Puff Pastry Dough Process, continued

⑩ Repeat the folds and square off the dough so that the edges are neat and uniform.

⑪ It's time to refrigerate the dough before rolling it out the final two times. Before wrapping it in plastic, put two finger indentations in the dough, pastry chef style, to indicated that this dough has had two turns. Once the dough has chilled for 1 hour in the fridge, repeat the process two more times. After you've made the last trifold, wrap the dough in plastic again and refrigerate it for at least 1 hour, or preferably overnight.

GLUTEN-FREE BAKING

A few excellent gluten-free flours have been on the market for a while now. The first was Cup4Cup, and this remains a reliable choice. King Arthur responded with Measure for Measure. You can also make your own gluten-free flour by combining rice flour, milk powder, soy flour, brown rice flour, and a pinch of xanthan gum. The recipe below will work with any of these flours. The lemon juice both seasons the dough and prevents oxidation.

Gluten-Free Dough

9¾ ounces/275 grams gluten-free all-purpose flour (about 1¾ cups)
¾   teaspoon xanthan gum
½   teaspoon/3 grams kosher salt
4   ounces/115 grams unsalted butter, cut into 1-inch/2.5-centimeter dice
1   large egg yolk
½   cup/120 milliliters water
1   tablespoon freshly squeezed lemon juice

1. Combine the flour, xanthan gum, and salt in a large bowl. Add the butter and toss the cubes until well coated. Press the flour into the butter with your hands until the butter chunks are about the size of peas.

2. In a small bowl, whisk together the egg yolk, water, and lemon juice and add to the flour mixture. Knead just until the dough comes together.

YIELD: 1¼ POUNDS/570 GRAMS DOUGH

The guinea fowl stew (page 53) with mushrooms and onions is ladled into a bowl and the baked lid is rested on top.

II

✳

THE SAVORY PIES

Pot Pies	44
Hand-Raised Pies	67
Rolled Raised Pies	83
Tarts and Galettes	103
Double-Crusted Pies	127
Turnovers	153
Vol-au-Vents	165

POT PIES

Chicken Pot Pie with Biscuit Crust	48
Beef Short Rib and Vegetable Pot Pie with Red Wine Sauce	51
Guinea Fowl Pot Pie	53
Roasted Vegetable Pot Pie	56
Wild Mushroom and Leek Pot Pie	57
Haddock, Corn, and Potato Pot Pie	59
Fish Pot Pie	60
Beef and Bone Marrow Pot Pie	61
Venison Pot Pie	64

This is the classic, unbeatable form of savory pie. And it's what we think of in America when we think about hot savory pies. In Britain, the term is rarely used, if ever. There's everything from a classic pork pie to a potato-covered stew (such as shepherd's pie or steak and kidney pie)—all simply referred to as pies. Elsewhere throughout the world pies take different shapes—moon pies in China, pastel de choclo in Peru, khachapuri in Georgia, or empanadas in Spain and Argentina. But here in the United States, the most popular form of savory pie is the chicken or beef pot pie.

We grew up eating Swanson pot pies, which came in a disposable aluminum pie plate and had both a bottom and a top crust—or as we call them here, double-crusted pies. But order a pot pie at a restaurant and most likely you'll receive an oven-proof dish filled with some form of stew covered with a golden brown crust on top. Depending on the restaurant, it might be fancy, like Brian's Guinea Fowl Pot Pie (page 53), or it might be a simple chicken pot pie. Or it might be vegetarian, such as a wild mushroom and leek pot pie. The top crust might vary, as does our chicken pot pie, which uses a biscuit crust.

The bottom line, though, is that a classic pot pie is nothing more than a stew, thickened with beurre manié or a cornstarch slurry (see page 46), covered with crust, and baked until the crust is browned and the stew is piping hot. Which makes the pot pie one of the most versatile and simple forms of savory pie there is.

You can create your own recipes when you know this. For a mushroom and leek pot pie, for instance, you would simply sauté mushrooms and leeks, deglaze with white wine, and add vegetable stock (along with, perhaps, fresh thyme or other herbs, some butter, perhaps a hit of lemon juice). Thicken the sauce, put it in your serving dish, and lay a sheet of puff pastry over it. (An actual recipe is on page 57.) We highly recommend you make the Blitz Puff Pastry Dough (page 36) at least once. It's a fascinating technique of creating a multilayered dough that puffs. But the quality of commercial puff pastry today is excellent, and no one we know will fault you for using store-bought puff pastry.

Pot pies can be a convenience food—if you make them ahead. They'll keep for a few days unbaked in your refrigerator, ready to pop in the oven. If you've made a Post-Thanksgiving Turkey Pot Pie (page 133) but can't eat another bite of turkey that weekend, freeze the pot pie for up to a month. You can also make pot pie in a pie plate or a cake pan. We love making individual pot pies in what are often called miniature casserole dishes. We use 2-cup/480-milliliter enameled cast-iron dishes for these.

Few dishes satisfy on a cold winter night the way a bubbling pot pie does.

Thickening Strategies

All of the pot pies require that you thicken the stew. If you don't add flour directly to the ingredients you're cooking (as is the case with the chicken pot pie), there are three basic methods of thickening stock to a rich sauce consistency: roux, beurre manié, and slurry. They all rely on the fact that starch granules, kept separate by water or fat, absorb liquid when hot. Their swelling is what does the thickening.

A slurry is the easiest and quickest: Mix enough water into cornstarch to achieve a cream-like consistency. Typically, you'll need equal parts cornstarch and water, combining them and stirring until the mixture is the consistency of heavy cream. Pour the slurry directly into hot liquid as needed. It takes only a moment for the starch to absorb the liquid, swell, and thicken the sauce, so add the slurry gradually until you achieve the consistency you want.

We prefer a flour-and-fat thickener, either roux or beurre manié, because the butter is an enricher. Roux is cooked and therefore superior to beurre manié, in which the flour is raw. But in small quantities, beurre manié is perfectly fine.

To make beurre manié, combine 2 tablespoons room-temperature butter with 2 tablespoons flour. Knead the two together with a fork or a spoon until you have a uniform paste. Add it in increments to prevent overthickening your sauce.

For a roux, we use a little more flour than butter, as flour is lighter than butter—so 2 tablespoons butter and 3 tablespoons flour. Melt the butter in a small saucepan over medium-high heat. Allow some of the water to bubble off. Add the flour and stir to combine. Cook more for a richer flavor if you wish. Cooking the roux until it's brown results in a nutty, flavorful roux, which is highly desirable when making a hearty stew such as gumbo. For smaller thickening quantities, using a pale, or blond, roux is fine. Also the more you cook a roux, the browner it gets—and the less thickening power it will have.

Both roux and beurre manié can be made in batches and kept refrigerated so that you always have some thickener on hand. Make a cup of beurre manié, roll it into a cylinder with plastic wrap, and refrigerate. Cut off disks as needed for thickening any and all sauces.

Chicken pot pie with a biscuit crust (page 48) is one of our favorites. And you can make it any way you wish. For the photo shoot we made individual pies in 4-inch/10-centimeter soufflé dishes. You could also put the filling in a pie plate and cover the top with biscuits. You might even do this in a rectangular baking dish. It's all the same, a creamy rich stew of chicken and vegetables. The thyme-infused cream is a great touch. And Brian worked overtime, using a mix of bread and pastry flours, to create a fabulous, high-rising biscuit dough.

Chicken Pot Pie
with Biscuit Crust

This is a classic chicken pot pie method, but instead of a full crust on top, we use biscuits. We prefer this method because it allows for a more elegant presentation. We also love the pleasure of the biscuits themselves. (These biscuits are especially tender because of the use of both bread and pastry flours, as well as minimal mixing, but it's fine to use all-purpose flour if that's what you have on hand.) Chicken and biscuits go well together, but this biscuit crust can be used to top any pie you wish—not just chicken. One thing to keep in mind is that a biscuit crust doesn't completely seal in the stew, so there will be a little more reduction during the cooking than with a full crust top.

The chicken stew—with diced carrot, celery, onion, and chicken stock—is thickened with flour (it should be very thick) and enriched by thyme-infused cream. We love to use shiitake mushrooms, cut large, but any mushroom will work here. The filling mixture is simmered on the stovetop to thicken it and cook out the roux. It's then cooled before being assembled; otherwise the biscuit dough can get soggy.

This is a superb meal to make from a supermarket rotisserie chicken, which gives you the right amount of meat for the pie and, for the ambitious cook, the carcass to make a stock from while you make the biscuits and stew.

1 cup/240 milliliters heavy cream
1 bunch thyme
10 whole black peppercorns, toasted and lightly cracked
1 bay leaf
2 ounces/60 grams unsalted butter, plus melted butter for brushing the biscuits
½ cup/65 grams small-diced onion
½ cup/50 grams small-diced celery
½ cup/50 grams small-diced carrot
   Kosher salt and freshly ground black pepper to taste
1 cup/60 grams sliced or quartered mushrooms
2 tablespoons all-purpose flour
1 cup/240 milliliters warm chicken stock, or more as needed
3 cups/675 grams chopped or shredded cooked chicken, preferably a mix of white and dark meat
1 cup/135 grams peas, thawed if frozen
   Juice of ½ lemon
1 recipe Biscuit Crust (recipe follows)

1. Combine the cream, thyme, peppercorns, and bay leaf in a small pot and bring to a boil over high heat. Remove from the heat and allow to cool.

2. In a large, heavy-bottomed saucepan, melt the butter over medium-high heat. Add the onion, celery, and carrot, salt them well, and cook until slightly soft, 3 to 5 minutes. Add the mushrooms and cook until they release their water, 5 minutes or so. Stir in the flour and cook for a couple minutes, just until the flour is distributed but not browned.

3. Add the warm chicken stock to the cream, then pour this mixture through a sieve into the pan of vegetables. Bring to a simmer, then reduce the heat to low and cook, stirring frequently, for 20 to 30 minutes. If it is very thick, you may need to add more stock.

4. Gently fold in the chicken and peas, then add the lemon juice and season with more salt (if needed) and pepper. Allow the filling to cool to room temperature, then cover and refrigerate until chilled, or up to 3 days.

5. Preheat the oven to 425°F/220°C. Line a rimmed baking sheet with aluminum foil or parchment paper.

6. Transfer the chicken mixture to a pie plate or similarly sized casserole dish, one just large enough to top with biscuits packed as tightly as possible. Arrange the biscuits on top and brush the biscuits with melted butter. Alternatively, you can make individual pot pies in ramekins, placing one biscuit on top of each.

7. Place the baking dish or ramekins on the lined baking sheet and bake until the stew is bubbling hot and the biscuits are nicely browned, 20 to 25 minutes for individual pies or 40 to 45 minutes for one large pie. Let sit for 10 minutes or so before serving.

SERVES 4

Biscuit Crust

4 ounces/115 grams bread flour (about 1 cup)
6 ounces/170 grams pastry flour (about 1⅓ cups)
1 tablespoon baking powder
1 teaspoon/5 grams kosher salt
3½ ounces/100 grams unsalted butter, diced and set out at room temperature for 30 minutes
¾ cup plus 2 tablespoons/200 milliliters buttermilk
Freshly ground black pepper to taste

1. Sift the flours, baking powder, and salt into a large bowl. Add the butter and mix by hand, pressing the butter and flour together until it resembles coarse meal. Add the buttermilk and a pinch of pepper and mix until just combined.

2. Transfer the dough to a floured work surface and roll out to about ⅓ inch/8.5 millimeters thick. Fold the dough into thirds as you would a letter. Roll it out again and repeat the folding and rolling out two more times.

3. Using a 3-inch/7.5-centimeter biscuit cutter or drinking glass, cut out as many biscuits as you can. There's usually enough trim from cutting to roll out and cut another biscuit. If not using right away, cover the biscuits until ready to assemble the pie.

Beef Short Rib and Vegetable Pot Pie
with Red Wine Sauce

This is a deeply soothing beef pot pie using gelatin-rich short ribs and red wine. Any stewing beef will work here, but the meat that comes from crosscut short ribs, the end of the ribs close to the belly, results in an especially delicious stew. The ribs (and the bones) are rich in connective tissue, which dissolves into gelatin, giving the stew depth and body. Using store-bought beef stock is fine, but if you make your own stock, this pie is especially fine. And if you're the sort who keeps some brown veal stock on hand, add it here and the pie will be incomparable.

2.2 pounds/1 kilogram bone-in crosscut beef
    short ribs
    Kosher salt and freshly ground black pepper
    to taste
¼ cup/30 grams all-purpose flour, plus more for
    dredging
    Vegetable oil, for browning the meat
1 cup/120 grams diced onion
½ cup/60 grams diced carrot
½ cup/60 grams diced celery
3 garlic cloves, peeled and smashed
2 tablespoons tomato paste
1½ cups/360 milliliters dry red wine
1 pound/450 grams diced fresh tomatoes

3 cups/700 milliliters veal or beef stock
½ bunch fresh thyme
12 whole black peppercorns
2 bay leaves
2 tablespoons red wine vinegar
1 large russet potato, peeled and cut into
    ½-inch/1.25-centimeter dice
3 thick slices bacon, cut crosswise into ¼-inch/
    6-millimeter strips
4 medium carrots, cut into ½-inch/1.25-
    centimeter dice
1 medium onion, cut into ½-inch/1.25-
    centimeter dice
2 tablespoons beurre manié or cornstarch slurry
    (see page 46), or as needed
12 ounces/340 grams Blitz Puff Pastry Dough
    (page 36) or 2 sheets store-bought puff pastry,
    thawed in the refrigerator
    Egg Wash (page 28)

1. Preheat the oven to 325°F/160°C.

2. Season the ribs all over with salt and pepper, then dredge in flour.

3. Pour enough oil into a large Dutch oven to cover the bottom by about ¼ inch/6 millimeters and heat over medium-high heat. When the oil is hot, brown the ribs on all sides. Transfer to a plate lined with paper towels.

4. Pour off the excess oil from the Dutch oven. (If the flour has burned, wipe out the pot and add a thin coat of fresh vegetable oil for sautéing.) Put the pot over medium heat and, when the oil is hot, add the onion, celery, carrot, and garlic and cook until tender, about 5 minutes. Turn the heat up to medium-high and continue to cook until the vegetables are browned, about 5 minutes. Clear a spot in the center of the pot and add the tomato paste so that it cooks and browns on the hot surface.

(recipe continues)

This **individual beef pot pie** is topped with the Blitz Puff Pastry Dough (page 36). You can see how flaky it is. You can also see how rich and enticing the stew below it looks, with the beef, carrot, and bacon lardons.

5. Deglaze the pan with half of the wine, then allow it to reduce to a syrup, 6 to 8 minutes. Add the remaining wine and allow this to reduce to a syrup, 6 to 8 minutes. Add the flour and stir it into the vegetables. Add the tomatoes, stock, thyme, peppercorns, bay leaves, and vinegar and bring it to a simmer.

6. Add the short ribs, cover the pot, and put it in the oven for 2 to 3 hours, until the meat is tender.

7. While the beef is braising, put the diced potato in a small pot, cover with cold water, and bring to a boil. Turn the heat down and simmer until tender, 10 to 15 minutes. Drain and set aside.

8. In a thick-bottomed sauté pan, cook the bacon over medium-high heat until slightly crisp, about 10 minutes, then add the carrots and onion and cook until the vegetables are tender, about 5 minutes; set aside.

9. When the ribs are done, transfer them to a plate. When the ribs are cool enough to handle, remove and discard the bones and any heavy sinew. Cut the meat into 1-inch/2.5-centimer pieces.

10. Strain the beef braising liquid into a medium saucepan. Bring it to a simmer and taste it. If you would like a stronger flavor, reduce the sauce. Add salt and pepper as necessary. The sauce should be thick enough to coat the meat. If it's not, thicken with beurre manié or a cornstarch slurry. Remove the pan from the heat and let the sauce cool.

11. Combine the cooled sauce with the diced meat, potato, and bacon-carrot-onion mixture. The filling must be cool or even cold, as heat might make the dough sag.

12. Preheat the oven to 375°F/190°C.

13. Fill four 2-cup/480-milliliter ovenproof dishes with the meat mixture.

14. Roll the puff pastry out to ⅛ inch/3 millimeters thick. Cut four circles from the puff pastry that are ½ inch/1.25 centimeters larger than the baking dishes. For each pie, egg wash one side of the pastry circle and place that side down on top of the dish, pressing the dough to seal it around the edges.

15. Egg wash the top and refrigerate the pies for 20 minutes, then egg wash a second time. Snip vent holes with a pair of scissors or a knife.

16. Bake until the crust is brown and the filling is hot, 30 to 40 minutes.

SERVES 4

Guinea Fowl Pot Pie

Brian's first chef de cuisine job, after five years of training under Master Chef Milos Cihelka, was at the Lark in Detroit in 1986. Although the restaurant was considered one of the best in the state, Brian's new boss wanted him to do at least one dish a night of "cuisine bourgeois," or peasant-style cooking. The idea was to show that all food, not just classical French cuisine, can be elevated, that all food has soul and you just have to find it. One of Brian's favorite creations was this guinea fowl pie.

It's a classic, modern pot pie with a puff pastry lid. And everything can be done ahead, with all components being reheated just before serving. You even bake the puff pastry in advance, and simply place it on top of the bowl to serve. This allows the pastry to stay crisp and flaky.

Guinea hens do more walking than flying, so the legs and thighs are better braised while the breast is best barded with fat and roasted separately. You can sometimes find them at farmers' markets, and they can be ordered from D'Artagnan and other online retail sources.

2 guinea hens, 2½ to 3 pounds/1.15 to 1.35 kilograms each
Kosher salt and freshly ground black pepper to taste
8 slices bacon
6 tablespoons/90 milliliters vegetable oil
2 cups/240 grams medium-diced onion
2 cups/360 grams large-diced pear
3 tablespoons chopped garlic
¾ cup/180 milliliters dry white wine
1½ cups/360 milliliters chicken stock
2 bay leaves
1 bunch fresh thyme
10 whole black peppercorns
4 ounces/112 grams pearl onions, unpeeled
3 tablespoons unsalted butter
8 ounces/225 grams wild mushrooms (such as chanterelle, cremini, and/or oyster)
¼ cup cornstarch slurry (see page 46), or as needed
4 Baked Puff Pastry Rounds (recipe follows)

1. Preheat the oven to 325°F/160°C.

2. Remove the legs and thighs from the birds, leaving the breasts on the rib cage. Season the breasts and dark meat all over with salt and pepper. Wrap each breast with 4 bacon slices and tie with butcher's twine. Set aside.

3. In a heavy bottomed, oven-proof skillet, heat 3 tablespoons oil over medium-high heat. When hot, brown the legs and thighs on all sides, about 4 minutes a side. Transfer to a plate. To the pan, add the onion, pear, and garlic and sauté until golden, about 5 minutes, then deglaze with the wine and reduce by half, 5 to 8 minutes. Add the stock, bring it to a simmer, and return the legs and thighs to the pan, along with the bay leaves, thyme, and peppercorns. Return to a simmer, cover, and put it in the oven until the meat is tender, about 1½ hours.

4. While the meat is braising, put the pearl onions in a small saucepan, cover with water, and bring to a boil. Simmer until tender, about 20 minutes—there should be no crunch. Drain. When cool enough to handle, peel and set aside.

(recipe continues)

5. Melt the butter in a large skillet over medium-high heat. Add the mushrooms and sauté until soft, about 5 minutes. Set aside.

6. When the meat is tender, transfer to a plate. Strain the braising liquid into a medium saucepan. Turn the oven temperature up to 375°F/190°C.

7. When the legs and thighs are cool enough to handle, pick the meat from the skin and bones and cut into 1-inch/2.5-centimeter pieces. Transfer to a bowl, add the pearl onions and mushrooms, and set aside.

8. Heat the remaining 3 tablespoons oil in a large, oven-proof skillet over medium-high heat. When the oil is hot, brown the breasts on both sides, about 3 minutes. Put the pan in the oven and cook to an internal temperature of 160°F/70°C, 20 to 25 minutes. Allow to rest for 10 minutes.

9. Bring the strained cooking liquid to a simmer. Slowly add the cornstarch slurry to the simmering liquid while stirring, until it thickens enough to heavily coat all the ingredients evenly. Add the dark meat mixture and toss gently until piping hot.

10. Remove and discard the twine and bacon from the breasts. Remove the meat from the skin and bones and cut into ¼-inch/6-millimeter slices.

11. Fill a 10-inch/25-centimeter straight-sided baking dish with the dark meat mixture. Top the stew with the sliced white meat and cover with a pastry lid.

SERVES 4

Baked Puff Pastry Rounds

12 ounces/340 grams Blitz Puff Pastry Dough (page 36) *or* 2 sheets store-bought puff pastry, thawed in the refrigerator
Egg Wash (page 28)

1. Preheat the oven to 375°F/190°C. Line a rimmed baking sheet with parchment paper.

2. Roll the puff pastry out to ⅛ inch/3 millimeters thick. Cut four circles from the puff pastry that are slightly larger than your serving dishes. Place the dough rounds on the lined baking sheet. Brush with egg wash, refrigerate for 15 minutes, then egg wash again.

3. Bake for 10 minutes, or until the tops are golden brown. Turn the oven temperature down to 325°F/160°C, crack open the oven door, and continue baking until the dough is cooked all the way through, 12 to 15 minutes.

4. Set aside at room temperature until ready to use.

Notice the bird on the lid of Brian's restaurant-style **guinea fowl pot pie**. To make a decorative lid, Brian finds an image, usually from the internet, prints it out, cuts it out, lays it on a sheet of dough, and cuts the shape using his template. If you want to try this, egg wash the lid and place the decorative piece on top, then egg wash just the chicken and refrigerate. Egg wash the entire lid again, then bake.

Roasted Vegetable Pot Pie

This vegetarian pie combines the sweetness of root vegetables with the savoriness of mushrooms. Roasting the onion, carrot, and cauliflower, whole or in large pieces, until caramelized really helps develop their natural flavors. For a different version of this dish, replace the cream with oat milk. For a little more depth, trade in chicken or beef stock for the vegetable stock. (Sorry, you can't make it vegan, as all of the doughs contain butter!)

- 6 ounces/165 grams small whole carrots, peeled and trimmed
- 6 ounces/165 grams large cauliflower florets
- 6 ounces/165 grams onion, cut into 4 wedges
- 4 tablespoons/60 milliliters olive oil
  Kosher salt and freshly ground black pepper to taste
- 4 ounces/110 grams broccoli rabe
- 1 cup/140 grams medium-diced russet potato
- 8 ounces/225 grams button mushrooms, quartered
- 1 tablespoon chopped garlic
- 1 cup/240 milliliters vegetable stock
- ½ cup/120 milliliters heavy cream
- 2 tablespoons cornstarch slurry (see page 46), or as needed
- 2 tablespoons chopped fresh tarragon
- 2 tablespoons chopped fresh flat-leaf parsley
- 6 ounces/170 grams Blitz Puff Pastry Dough (page 36) or 1 sheet store-bought puff pastry, thawed in the refrigerator
  Egg Wash (page 28)

1. Preheat the oven to 375°F/190°C. Line a rimmed baking sheet with aluminum foil.

2. Put the carrots, cauliflower, and onion on the lined baking sheet and drizzle with 2 tablespoons oil. Lightly toss to distribute the oil, then spread out the vegetables in a single layer. Roast until all are golden brown and soft, 20 to 30 minutes. Leave the oven on.

3. Meanwhile, bring a pot of salted water to a boil, add the broccoli rabe, and blanch until tender, about 10 minutes. Transfer to a large bowl of ice water to stop the cooking process, drain again, and set aside.

4. Put the potato in the same pot, cover with cold water, and bring to a boil. Turn the heat down and simmer until tender, 15 to 20 minutes. Drain.

5. Heat the remaining 2 tablespoons oil in a large sauté pan over medium-high heat. Add the mushrooms and cook until browned, 6 to 8 minutes, then add the garlic cook until just soft, about 2 minutes. Transfer to a large bowl.

6. In a small saucepan, bring the stock to a boil, then whisk in the cream. Turn the heat down to a simmer and reduce the stock by a third. Season with salt and pepper. Thicken with a cornstarch slurry so that the sauce coats the ingredients evenly. Allow it to cool completely, then fold in the chopped herbs.

7. Cut the roasted vegetables and broccoli rabe into 1-inch/2.5-centimeter pieces and add to the bowl of mushrooms and garlic. Add the cream sauce. There should be enough to moisten and coat all the vegetables well.

8. Divide the vegetable stew mixture into four 2-cup/480-milliliter ovenproof dishes.

9. Roll out the puff pastry to ⅛ inch/3 millimeters thick. Cut four circles from the puff pastry that are ½ inch/1.25 centimeters larger than your baking dishes. For each pie, egg wash one side of the pastry circle and place that side down on top of the ramekin, pressing the dough to seal it around the edges. Egg wash the top and refrigerate for 15 minutes, then egg wash again. With the tip of a sharp knife, cut an X in the center of the dough so the filling can vent.

10. Bake until the dough is brown and crispy and the filling is hot, 20 to 30 minutes.

SERVES 4

Wild Mushroom and Leek Pot Pie

This is a fabulous vegetarian pot pie, with leeks, mushrooms, stock, wine, and cream. It's especially good if you use wild, meaty mushrooms, such as chanterelles, morels, or hedgehog mushrooms, but if you have access only to domesticated mushrooms, a mix of portobello, cremini, and stemmed shiitakes will work. Use white button mushrooms only as a last resort. If you want more heft, diced potato can be included in the stew.

- 2 tablespoons unsalted butter
- 1 large leek (about 8 ounces/225 grams), halved lengthwise, cleaned, and thinly sliced crosswise
  Kosher salt and freshly ground black pepper to taste
- 1 cup/240 milliliters heavy cream
- 2 tablespoons vegetable oil
- 1 pound/450 grams assorted wild mushrooms
- ¼ cup/40 grams minced shallot
- ½ cup/120 milliliters dry sherry
- 3 tablespoons all-purpose flour
- 1 cup/240 milliliters vegetable stock
- 2 tablespoons chopped fresh flat-leaf parsley
- 1 tablespoon chopped fresh thyme leaves
- 1 tablespoon chopped fresh tarragon
- 6 ounces/170 grams Blitz Puff Pastry Dough (page 36) or 1 sheet store-bought puff pastry, thawed in the refrigerator
  Egg Wash (page 28)

1. Melt the butter in a large saucepan over low heat. Add the leek, season with salt and pepper, cover, and cook just to soften, being careful to not let the leek brown. Add the cream and bring to a boil, then reduce the heat and simmer until the leek is completely tender and the cream has thickened slightly, about 5 minutes. Remove the pan from the heat.

2. In a large sauté pan, heat the oil over high heat. When the oil is smoking hot, add just enough mushrooms to loosely cover the bottom without crowding. Press down on them with a spatula to sear them for flavor, then transfer to a bowl. Continue until you've cooked all the mushrooms, then return all of them to the pan, turn the heat down to medium, and add the shallot. Cook until the shallot is translucent, 3 to 4 minutes, then deglaze the pan with the sherry. Simmer and reduce until the pan is almost dry, 6 to 8 minutes. Stir in the flour. When it's well distributed, add the stock, bring to a boil, and allow to thicken for 4 to 5 minutes. Add the creamed leek and check the seasoning, adding more salt or pepper as needed. Remove the pan from the heat and set aside to cool, then fold in the fresh herbs.

3. Preheat the oven to 375°F/190°C.

4. Fill four 2-cup/480-milliliter ovenproof dishes with the mushroom mixture.

5. Roll the puff pastry out to ⅛ inch/3 millimeters thick. Cut four circles from the puff pastry that are ½ inch/1.25 centimeters larger than the baking dishes. For each pie, egg wash one side of the pastry circle and place that side down on top of the dish, pressing the dough to seal it around the edges. Egg wash the top, refrigerate for 15 minutes, then egg wash again.

6. Bake until the crust is golden and the filling is hot all the way through, about 30 minutes. Allow the pies to rest for 15 minutes or so before serving.

SERVES 4

Haddock, Corn, and Potato Pot Pie

Any soup can be made into a stew, and any stew can be made into a pot pie. When Brian was thinking about possible seafood pies, his mind went first to a chowder using haddock or cod. Corn and potato are terrific additions to chowder and, with the bacon, go great with this fish. When poaching fish, never exceed 180°F/82°C; the liquid should not even simmer (simmering happens at around 185°F/85°C). This is especially important with haddock, as it is very flaky when cooked. Try to keep the pieces of fish big and identifiable but still able to fit on a spoon.

- 1 cup/140 grams medium-diced russet potato
- 3 ounces/80 grams bacon, cut into ¼-inch/ 6-millimeter strips
- 4 ounces/120 grams button mushrooms, quartered
- ½ cup/75 grams fresh corn cut off the cob
- 1 cup/240 milliliters fish or chicken stock
- ½ cup/120 milliliters heavy cream
- 12 ounces/340 grams haddock or cod
- 2 tablespoons cornstarch slurry (see page 46), or as needed
- ¼ cup/15 grams chopped fresh herbs (such as chives, flat-leaf parsley, and/or tarragon)
- 6 ounces/170 grams Blitz Puff Pastry Dough (page 36) or 1 sheet store-bought puff pastry, thawed in the refrigerator
  Egg Wash (page 28)

1. Preheat the oven to 375°F/190°C.

2. Put the potato in a small pot, cover with cold water, and bring to a boil. Turn the heat down and simmer just until tender, 10 to 15 minutes. Drain.

3. In a large skillet, cook the bacon over medium heat until the fat has rendered and the bacon is gently crispy, 7 to 8 minutes. Add the mushrooms and cook until softened but not browned, 3 to 5 minutes. Add the corn, stock, and cream and bring to a simmer. Turn the heat down so that the liquid is below a simmer and add the fish. Cook until the fish is heated through, about 5 minutes.

4. Using a lid, drain off as much liquid as you can into a saucepan, keeping the solids in the skillet. Bring the liquid to a simmer and thicken with the cornstarch slurry. It should coat the back of a spoon. Add the solids from the skillet to the thickened sauce, along with the herbs, and combine all the ingredients. Fill four 2-cup/480-milliliter ovenproof dishes with the mixture.

5. Roll out the puff pastry to ⅛ inch/3 millimeters thick. Cut four circles from the puff pastry that are ½ inch/1.25 centimeters larger than the baking dishes. For each pie, egg wash one side of the pastry circle and place that side down on top of the dish, pressing the dough to seal it around the edges. Egg wash the top and snip vent holes with a pair of scissors or cut them with a knife. For a deeper finish, refrigerate the pies for 15 minutes and egg wash a second time.

6. Bake until the crust is golden and the filling is hot, about 30 minutes.

SERVES 4

This is a pie meant to be served family style, each person serving themselves some chowder-like stew and some crust.

Fish Pot Pie

Any professional chef will agree that not wasting anything is not only one key to financial success, it's also a matter of respecting your ingredients. This pot pie came about as a great way for Brian to use trim pieces of fish and shellfish for a winter lunch special. But it's good enough to make in its own right, using any lean, white fish, such as cod, hake, or halibut. Here, the rich, creamy sauce is full of chunks of fish and is topped with whipped potatoes (they're finished with egg yolk for a light, airy top).

2.2 pounds/1 kilogram lean, white-fleshed fish
2 cups/480 milliliters milk
  Kosher salt and freshly ground black pepper to taste
½ cup/55 grams (1-inch/2.5-centimeter) pieces green beans
3 ounces/90 grams unsalted butter
⅓ cup/40 grams minced onion
⅔ cup/80 grams all-purpose flour
1 tablespoon Dijon mustard
  Grated fresh nutmeg to taste
2 tablespoons drained capers
3 tablespoons chopped fresh herbs (such as chervil, chives, and/or flat-leaf parsley)

FOR THE POTATO CRUST

1 pound/450 grams russet potatoes, peeled and cut into 2-inch/5-centimeter dice
2 tablespoons unsalted butter, softened
2 tablespoons heavy cream
1 large egg yolk
  Kosher salt and freshly ground black pepper to taste

1. Put the fish in a large sauté pan, add the milk, and gently simmer over medium heat until barely cooked through, 6 to 7 minutes. Using a slotted spoon or spatula, transfer the fish to a large bowl and set aside to cool. Return the pan of milk to the stove and keep warm over low heat, but do not let it boil.

2. Meanwhile, bring a pot of salted water to a boil, add the green beans, and blanch until tender, 5 to 6 minutes. Transfer to a large bowl of ice water to stop the cooking process, drain again, and set aside.

3. In a large, heavy-bottomed saucepan, melt the butter over medium heat. Add the onion and sauté until soft, 4 to 5 minutes. Add the flour to make a roux and cook for 2 to 3 minutes. Add the warm milk and whisk until smooth, then bring to a boil. Turn the heat down to a simmer and cook until there is about 1½ cups/360 milliliters of sauce, 20 to 30 minutes. Stir in the Dijon and season with salt, pepper, and nutmeg.

4. To the bowl of fish, add the capers, green beans, herbs, and sauce and toss gently. The sauce should be thick enough to coat everything. Transfer to a 10-inch/25-centimeter straight-sided baking dish. Cool to room temperature.

5. Preheat the oven to 375°F/190°C.

6. To make the potato crust, put the potatoes in a large pot, cover with cold water, and bring to a boil. Turn the heat down and simmer until completely soft, 15 to 20 minutes, then drain well. Transfer the potatoes to the bowl of an electric mixer fitted with the whip attachment and whip the potatoes; with the motor running, add the butter and cream and then the egg yolk, scraping down the sides to make sure there are no lumps. Season with salt and pepper.

7. Spread the whipped potatoes evenly over the seafood mixture.

8. Bake until hot all the way through and the crust is lightly browned, 30 to 35 minutes.

SERVES 6 TO 8

Beef and Bone Marrow Pot Pie

This is a very cool looking pie, a centerpiece with a marrow bone sticking out of dough, with a rich beef stew inside. You'll have to request that your butcher cut you a 5-inch/13-centimeter beef shank marrow bone. Be sure to stipulate how you're using it—it needs to stand upright, so it must have a clean base. You may need to scrape the bone clean with the back of a knife if there is sinew or membrane on it. Removing the membrane from the bone makes a better presentation; try soaking the bone in cold water for an hour to facilitate its removal. You'll want to serve this with an espresso spoon or any spoon small enough to scoop out the luscious marrow.

1 pound/450 grams lean beef chuck, cut into 1-inch/2.5-centimeter pieces
 Kosher salt and freshly ground black pepper to taste
2 tablespoons all-purpose flour, plus more for dredging
 Vegetable oil, for browning the meat
½ cup/60 grams small-diced onion
½ cup/60 grams diced carrot
½ cup/60 grams diced celery
3 garlic cloves, peeled and smashed
1 tablespoon tomato paste
½ cup/120 milliliters dry red wine
½ cup/90 grams diced fresh tomatoes
1 cup/240 milliliters veal or beef stock
½ bunch fresh thyme
6 whole black peppercorns
1 bay leaf
1 tablespoon red wine vinegar
1 cup/140 grams medium-diced russet potato
2 thick slices bacon, cut crosswise into ¼-inch/6-millimeter strips
2 tablespoons beurre manié or cornstarch slurry (see page 46), or as needed
1 (5-inch/13-centimeter) center-cut beef marrow bone, scraped clean (see headnote)
10 ounces/280 grams Pâte Brisée (page 33)
 Egg Wash (page 28)

1. Preheat the oven to 325°F/160°C.

2. Season the beef all over with salt and pepper, then dredge in flour.

3. Pour enough oil into a large Dutch oven to cover the bottom by about ¼ inch/8 millimeters and heat over medium-high heat. When the oil is hot, brown the beef on all sides. Transfer to a plate lined with paper towels.

4. Pour off the excess oil from the Dutch oven. (If the flour has burned, wipe out the pot and add a thin coat of fresh vegetable oil for sautéing.) Put the pot over medium heat and, when the oil is hot, add the onion, carrot, celery, and garlic and cook until tender, 8 to 10 minutes. Turn the heat up to medium-high and continue to cook until the vegetables are browned, about another 3 or 4 minutes. Clear a spot in center of the pot and add the tomato paste so that it cooks and browns on the hot surface.

5. Deglaze the pan with half of the red wine, then allow it to reduce to a syrup, 5 to 8 minutes. Add the remaining wine and allow this to reduce to a syrup, 5 to 8 minutes. Add the 2 tablespoons of flour and stir it into the vegetables. Add the tomatoes, stock, thyme, peppercorns, bay leaf, and vinegar and bring it to a simmer.

6. Add the browned beef, cover the pot, and put it in the oven for 2 to 3 hours, until the meat is tender.

7. While the beef is braising, put the diced potato in a small pot, cover with cold water, and bring to a boil. Turn the heat down and simmer until tender, about 15 minutes. Drain and set aside.

8. In a thick-bottomed sauté pan, cook the bacon over medium heat until slightly crisp, 7 to 8 minutes, then transfer to a plate lined with paper towels.

(recipe continues)

9. When the meat is tender, use a slotted spoon or tongs to transfer the pieces to a large bowl.

10. Strain the braising liquid into a medium saucepan. Bring it to a simmer and taste it. If you would like a stronger flavor, reduce the sauce. Add salt and pepper as necessary. The sauce should be thick enough to coat the meat. If it's not, thicken with beurre manié or a cornstarch slurry.

11. Add the beef, potato, and bacon to the sauce and mix well to coat everything evenly.

12. Preheat the oven to 375°F/190°C.

13. Stand the bone marrow on its end in the middle of a 9-inch/23-centimeter pie plate. Arrange the filling around the bone.

14. Roll out the pâte brisée into a circle about ⅛ inch/3 millimeters thick and about 1 inch/2.5 centimeters bigger than your pie plate. Cut an X directly in the center big enough that the bone will fit through. Place the dough on top of the pie with the bone sticking up through the X, trimming the dough as needed. Egg wash the top, refrigerate the pie for 15 minutes, then egg wash the top a second time.

15. Bake until the crust is brown and the filling is hot, 30 to 40 minutes.

SERVES 4

We love this pie for its dramatic presentation and delicious interior enriched with the marrow. When ordering marrow bones, make sure the butcher cuts the bone at a 90-degree angle so that it stands up in the pan. To construct the pie, stand the cleaned bone in the center of the dish. Spoon in the beef filling. Cut an X in the center of the dough circle that you're using for the lid. Lower the dough onto the bowl, with the bone sliding through the X. Be sure to provide small spoons so that you can scoop the marrow out as you eat the pot pie.

Venison Pot Pie

Game such as venison is lean, which makes it more difficult to cook. Special care must be taken with time and temperature so that it's succulent and delicious, and not dry. Trim all the fat from the venison; unlike beef fat, venison fat is waxy and unpalatable. Depending on the size of the animal, and whether it's harvested from the wild or farm-raised, there may not be much shoulder or breast meat. Choose your meat wisely, picking tougher cuts from the leg, which are best for braising.

1 cup/140 grams medium-diced russet potato
1 pound/450 grams venison, cut into 1-inch/
   2.5-centimeter pieces
   Kosher salt and freshly ground black pepper
   to taste
   All-purpose flour, for dredging
2 tablespoons olive oil
1 cup/120 grams small-diced onion
1 cup/120 grams small-diced celery
1 cup/120 grams small-diced carrot
3 garlic cloves, minced
2 tablespoons tomato paste
1 cup/240 milliliters dry red wine
2 cups/480 milliliters beef stock
½ bunch fresh thyme, tied
1 bay leaf
6 ounces/170 grams Blitz Puff Pastry Dough
   (page 36) or 1 sheet store-bought puff pastry,
   thawed in the refrigerator
   Egg Wash (page 28)
2 tablespoons cornstarch slurry or beurre manié
   (see page 46), or as needed
1 tablespoon balsamic vinegar

1. Put the potato in a small pot, cover with cold water, and bring to a boil. Turn the heat down and simmer until tender, 15 to 20 minutes. Drain and set aside.

2. Season the meat all over with salt and pepper, then dredge in flour. Heat the oil in a large, heavy-bottomed skillet over medium-high heat and brown the meat on all sides. Depending on the size of your skillet, you may have to do this in batches. Transfer the meat to a plate lined with paper towels. Reserve enough oil to cook the vegetables in.

3. Add the onion, celery, carrot, and garlic to the fat remaining in the skillet and sauté over medium-high heat until soft, 8 to 10 minutes. Stir in the tomato paste until it coats all the vegetables. Deglaze the pan with half of the wine, then allow it to reduce to a syrup, 5 to 10 minutes. Add the remaining wine and allow this to reduce to a syrup, about 5 minutes. Add the stock, thyme, and bay leaf and bring to a simmer. Add the meat, cover the pot, and cook at a very gentle simmer until the meat is tender, about 1½ hours. Remove the bay leaf and thyme.

4. Preheat the oven to 375°F/190°C. Line a rimmed baking sheet with parchment paper.

5. Roll out the pastry dough to a thickness of ⅛ inch/3 millimeters. Cut out a circle to fit the size of a 9-inch/23-centimeter pie plate. Put the dough on the lined baking sheet and cut out a small vent hole in the center. Egg wash the dough and refrigerate it for 15 minutes. Egg wash it a second time, then bake until golden and cooked through.

6. Using a slotted spoon or tongs, transfer the meat to a large bowl. Thicken the braising liquid with the cornstarch slurry or beurre manié until the sauce easily coats the ingredients, a few minutes. Return the meat to the sauce and add the vinegar. The sauce should be thick enough to coat the meat evenly.

7. Transfer the hot mixture to the pie plate and top with the golden-brown pastry.

SERVES 4

Making decorative crusts is easy thanks to the internet. For his **venison pot pie**, Brian googled images of antlers (the decoration should reflect what's in the pie), printed an image, then traced it. He cut it out, laid it on the dough, and cut out the antlers using a paring knife. He egg washed a puff pastry lid and laid the antlers on top. After a second egg wash, the pie lid was ready to bake.

HAND-RAISED PIES

Hot-Water Dough	70
Hand-Raised Pork Pies	70
Beef, Onion, and Ale Hand-Raised Pies	75
Chicken, Pork, Liver, and Mushroom Hand-Raised Pies	77
Chicken and Ham Hand-Raised Pies	80

This is the finished **Hand-Raised Pork Pie** (page 70), its deeply golden-brown color the result of the double egg wash.

Hand-raised pies are the quintessential British pie—individual pies that are molded by hand and most commonly filled with pork. They are some of the oldest pies in Great Britain, dating to the Middle Ages, a time before pie molds. In those early days, the dough likely would have been a flour and water crust not meant to be eaten; rather it was designed to be the cooking vessel and then the serving dish. The thick crust, well crimped and baked, would seal in the freshness and keep the meat from spoiling (it is in effect pasteurized within the dough).

Hand-raised pies can be eaten straight from the oven but are designed to be made ahead and eaten at room temperature. They're satisfying by themselves, but add a salad or some mashed potatoes and you have a meal.

Pork is the traditional filling, as it is fatty and inexpensive and delicious. But you can make individual hand-raised pies using just about any filling from the book you wish, provided it's not too liquidy (such as the filling for the pot pies, which would not do well here).

These pies are called "hand-raised" because traditionally the dough is shaped on what's called a pie dolly, a wooden cylinder about 3 inches/7.5 centimeters in diameter and 6 inches/15 centimeters tall with a handle. You simply press the floured dolly down into a piece of dough and, using your hands, raise the dough up the sides of the cylinder to a height of about 3 inches/7.5 centimeters. If you were simply to roll out the dough to the desired thinness and wrap it around the dolly, this would result in unappealingly thick folds. Pressing it up the dolly allows you to achieve the shape and thinness you want. (If you don't have a pie dolly, improvise with a mason jar or glass of similar dimensions.)

Hand-raised pies traditionally call for a hot-water dough, a dough that stays very crisp after cooking and also absorbs the juices from the meat. Put your flour in a bowl, melt the lard in water, dump it into the flour, and mix. This dough is by far the easiest dough to make but the trickiest to use, because you have to work with it at the right temperature, not too hot and not too cold. It's important to make the dough as thin as possible for even cooking and better eating. Brian loves the hot-water dough because even though it's a little harder to work with, it results in a better looking pie.

These are fun hand pies to make and to serve. We begin with the recipe for hot-water dough, then the pies: first a traditional pork pie, and then some options.

Making the crust for hand-raised pies. The base of the individual pie is formed by shaping a 6-ounce/170-gram ball of hot-water dough (the two balls on the right) using a floured pie dolly, or similarly shaped cylinder, to form a cup. A 2-ounce/60-gram piece of dough (the two balls on the left) is flattened by hand to serve as the lid.

Hot-Water Dough

All of the pies in this chapter use the same dough recipe. It's easily the fastest dough to make, but you have to work with it when it's at the right temperature. After it comes together, wrap it in plastic and let it rest for 30 minutes before bringing out the pie dolly (or whatever you're using as a mold—a glass, a jar, for instance).

Brian wasn't happy with the standard hot-water dough—a little tough, a little dry. He consulted Calum Franklin's dough, which includes egg. Sure enough, two eggs did the trick. Brian also infuses the water-lard mixture with thyme for extra flavor.

    6 ounces/170 grams lard
 ½ bunch fresh thyme sprigs
    1 cup/240 milliliters water
 20 ounces/560 grams bread flour
 ½ teaspoon/4 grams salt
    2 eggs, beaten

1. Combine the lard, thyme, and water in a saucepan and bring to a simmer to melt the lard. Remove from the heat. Set aside and allow the thyme to infuse the liquid, 10 minutes or so.

2. Sift the flour and salt into the bowl of a stand mixer fitted with the paddle attachment. Turn the mixer to medium speed and slowly add the eggs. Mix for 2 to 3 minutes.

3. Remove the herbs from the liquid, place it back on the heat, and bring to a simmer. Add half the liquid while the machine is running on low. Stop, scrape down the sides, then lower the mixer back to low and add the remaining liquid. Mix just until the dough comes together.

4. Cover with plastic wrap, cool to room temperature, then refrigerate at least 30 minutes or until ready to use. If the dough is thoroughly chilled, allow it to rest at room temperature until it's pliable, 30 to 40 minutes.

YIELD: 2 POUNDS/920 GRAMS DOUGH (enough for a 6-ounce/170-gram bottom and a 2-ounce/60-gram top for each of four pies)

Hand-Raised Pork Pies

The filling for this traditional pie is kind of a cross between a country sausage and pâté, with the roasted garlic giving it a little more depth. This is a pie meant to be served hot from the oven.

    2 tablespoons unsalted butter
 ½ cup/60 grams small-diced onion
 ½ cup/60 grams quartered mushrooms
1½ pounds/720 grams coarsely ground pork
    6 ounces/170 grams Canadian bacon or ham, medium-diced
    2 tablespoons roasted garlic (see Note)
    1 large egg
    1 tablespoon kosher salt
    1 teaspoon freshly ground black pepper
 ½ teaspoon grated fresh nutmeg
 ¼ teaspoon cayenne
    2 pounds/920 grams Hot-Water Dough (*left*), freshly made and allowed to cool slightly
       All-purpose flour, for dusting
       Egg Wash (page 28)

1. In a medium skillet, melt the butter over medium-high heat. Add the onion and mushrooms, cover the pan, and cook until soft, 3 to 4 minutes. Transfer to a large bowl and allow to cool.

2. Add the ground pork, bacon, roasted garlic, egg, salt, pepper, nutmeg, and cayenne and thoroughly mix by hand using a tiger claw method (stiffen your fingers into a claw), vigorously mixing it all until the meat is sticky. Cover the mixture and refrigerate it.

3. When the dough is cool enough to handle, weigh out four 6-ounce/170-gram pieces and four 2-ounce/60-gram pieces. Shape the larger pieces into disks about the size of your pie dolly or mold, about 3 by ½ inch/7.5 by 1.25 centimeters. Press the smaller pieces into lids ⅛ to ¼ inch thick and the diameter of your pie dolly or mold. Refrigerate the pieces until they're cool and stiff but not solid, about 15 minutes. If the dough is too warm, it will not hold the shape of the pie dolly.

4. Begin shaping the larger disks into cups the size of your pie dolly or mold. The dough should be pliable and shouldn't crack as your hands warm it. Flour a pie dolly or mold and add some flour to the center of the first piece of dough so that the bottom of the pie dolly doesn't stick to the dough, then press the dolly into the center of the dough. Using your fingers, and with your thumbs on the top of the dolly, press the dough up around the dolly. Bring the dough about 3 inches/7.5 centimeters up the sides, checking regularly that the dolly isn't sticking to the dough. Transfer the dough, a 3-inch/7.5 centimeter cup, to a rimmed baking sheet and refrigerate it while you shape and chill the remaining three large pieces.

5. Preheat the oven to 375°F/190°C.

6. Remove the chilled dough cups from the fridge. Fill them almost all the way to the top with the chilled meat mixture.

7. Press the smaller dough pieces into disks to fit the bottoms as lids, making a little ridge around the edges to prepare them for crimping. Moisten the edges of one lid and pinch it all around the cup to seal it. Do the same for the remaining lids.

8. Lightly brush the tops with egg wash, being careful not to let it pool. Crimp the edges of each pie using the three-finger method (see page 30), or crimp as desired. Use a knife or scissors to cut slits in the pie lids. Refrigerate for at least 15 minutes (or as long as overnight), then egg wash a second time.

9. Bake the pies until the internal temperature reaches 150°F/65°C, 45 to 60 minutes. Allow to rest for at least 15 minutes before serving.

SERVES 4

> *Note:* Several of our fillings include roasted garlic, which adds a sweet garlicky note to the forcemeat. It's a simple and delicious seasoning and all-around excellent condiment.
>
> *To roast garlic:* Rub a whole head of garlic with vegetable oil. Wrap the garlic in aluminum foil, place it in a small baking pan, and roast at 375°F/190°C until the garlic is soft, about 20 minutes. Unwrap and allow it to cool, then slice off the top of the head and squeeze out the garlic. Use as instructed, or store in a covered container in the fridge for up to 1 week.

① To make the hot-water dough for hand-raised pies, lard is melted in hot water, which is then added to the flour mixture. The first step is to flour your pie dolly to facilitate removing the dough.

② This photo shows two different sized balls of dough. The large balls will become the bases of the pies. The smaller balls are lids that you will flatten by hand. Press the pie dolly into the larger dough ball, and raise it up along the sides of the dolly.

③ It sometimes helps to invert the pie dolly and work the dough down the pie dolly.

④ Shape the meat filling into a ball the diameter of the dough cup you've shaped on the dolly and put it into the dough cup. The critical part here is to avoid any air pockets.

⑤ Pat the meat down so that the surface is flat and about ½ inch/1.25 centimeters below the top edge of the dough cup.

⑥ Enclose the meat in the dough. Wet the outer edge of the dough lid with water, place it on the meat, and press it down, then pinch the top and the cup together to seal it firmly.

⑦ To crimp the dough, pinch six points. Start by pinching the dough on either side to create two points, rotate the pie 45 degrees, and make two more pinches. Turn the dough again to create the final two points, for a kind of crown shape.

⑧ Egg wash the pie as evenly as possible, being careful not to allow egg wash to pool in the creases on top. Refrigerate the pie for 15 minutes, egg wash again, and it's ready to bake.

Beef, Onion, and Ale Hand-Raised Pies

The filling for these pies has to be fully cooked and cooled, so it's best to make it a day in advance. It's a terrific all-purpose filling that would be great as a turnover or even a large pot pie; just cut the beef into pieces appropriate for the size of the crust you're filling. Use a dark ale or stout because it goes well with the mustard's heat and sweetness from the onions. Avoid using the popular American IPAs—they'll make the end sauce a touch bitter.

1½ pounds/675 grams beef chuck or brisket, trimmed and cut into 1-inch/2.5-centimeter pieces
    Kosher salt and freshly ground black pepper to taste
2 tablespoons all-purpose flour, plus more for dredging
2 tablespoons olive oil
1 pound/450 grams onions, cut into short julienne
2 tablespoons minced garlic
1 tablespoon Colman's mustard powder
3 thyme sprigs
1 bay leaf
1½ cups/360 milliliters dark ale
1 cup/240 milliliters beef stock
¼ cup/60 milliliters Worcestershire sauce
2 tablespoons beurre manié (see page 46), or as needed
2 pounds/920 grams Hot-Water Dough (page 70), freshly made and allowed to cool slightly
    Egg Wash (page 28)

1. Season the beef all over with salt and pepper, then dredge in flour.

2. Heat the oil in a large, heavy-bottomed skillet over medium-high heat. When the oil is hot, add the beef and brown evenly on all sides, a few minutes per side. Transfer the meat to a large bowl. Add the onions and garlic, cover, turn the heat down to medium, and cook until soft, 7 to 8 minutes. Remove the lid, turn the heat up to high, and continue cooking until the onions are caramelized and browned, 5 to 6 minutes.

3. Stir in the mustard, thyme, and bay leaf, then add the ale, bring to a boil, and reduce by half. Add the stock and Worcestershire and return the meat to the pan. Cover, turn the heat down to low, and simmer until the meat is fork-tender, about 1½ hours.

4. Using a slotted spoon or tongs, transfer the meat to a large bowl, turn the heat up to high, and bring the liquid to a boil. Whip in the beurre manié and cook until thick, 8 to 10 minutes. Return the meat to the sauce, remove from the heat, and cool to room temperature.

5. When the dough is cool enough to handle, weigh out four 6-ounce/170-gram pieces and four 2-ounce/60-gram pieces. Shape the larger pieces into disks about the size of your pie dolly or mold, about 3 by ½ inch/7.5 by 1.25 centimeters. Press the smaller pieces into lids ⅛ to ¼ inch thick and the diameter of your pie dolly or mold. Refrigerate the pieces until they're cool and stiff but not solid, about 15 minutes. If the dough is too warm, it will not hold the shape of the pie dolly.

(recipe continues)

The traditional **hand-raised beef, onion, and ale pie** is meant to be eaten hot. Some hot mushroom gravy (Mushroom Jus Lié, page 196) would go perfectly with this pie.

6. Begin shaping the larger disks into cups the size of your pie dolly or mold. The dough should be pliable and shouldn't crack as your hands warm it. Flour a pie dolly or mold and add some flour to the center of the first piece of dough so that the bottom of the pie dolly doesn't stick to the dough, then press the dolly into the center of the dough. Using your fingers, and with your thumbs on the top of the dolly, press the dough up around the dolly. Bring the dough about 3 inches/7.5 centimeters up the sides, checking regularly that the dolly isn't sticking to the dough. Transfer the dough, a 3-inch/7.5-centimeter cup, to a rimmed baking sheet and refrigerate it while you shape and chill the remaining three large pieces.

7. Preheat the oven to 375°F/190°C.

8. Remove the chilled dough cups from the fridge. Fill them almost all the way to the top with the cooled meat mixture.

9. Press the smaller dough pieces into disks to fit the bottoms as lids, making a little ridge around the edges to prepare them for crimping. Moisten the edges of one lid and pinch it all around the cup to seal it. Do the same for the remaining lids.

10. Lightly brush the tops with egg wash, being careful not to let it pool. Crimp the edges of each pie using the three-finger method (see page 30), or crimp as desired. Use a knife or scissors to cut slits in the pie lids. Refrigerate for at least 15 minutes (or as long as overnight), then egg wash a second time.

11. Bake the pies until the internal temperature reaches 150°F/65°C, 45 to 60 minutes. Allow to rest for at least 15 minutes before serving.

SERVES 4

Chicken, Pork, Liver, and Mushroom Hand-Raised Pies

These pies have a lot of chunky filling, and the pork sausage takes on the flavor of a sweet Madeira wine reduction. You can either fold everything into the pork for a random garnish effect or do layers: pork, chicken, pork, liver, pork, mushrooms, pork.

- 14 ounces/400 grams boneless, skinless chicken breast, cut into 1-inch/2.5-centimeter dice
- 4 ounces/112 grams cleaned chicken livers
  Kosher salt and freshly ground black pepper to taste
- 2 tablespoons olive oil
- 4 ounces/112 grams wild or domestic mushrooms, cut into large chunks
- 2 tablespoons minced shallot
- ½ cup/120 milliliters Madeira wine
- 1 pound/450 grams ground pork shoulder
- 1 large egg
- ¼ cup/60 milliliters heavy cream
- 2 pounds/920 grams Hot-Water Dough (page 70), freshly made and allowed to cool slightly
  Egg Wash (page 28)

1. Season the chicken breast and livers all over with salt and pepper.

2. Heat the oil in a large skillet over medium-high heat. Add the breast and brown on both sides, 2 to 3 minutes, then transfer to a large bowl. Add the livers and brown on both sides, 2 to 3 minutes, then transfer to a cutting board. Add the mushrooms and cook until soft, 7 to 8 minutes, then transfer to the bowl with the chicken. Add the shallot and Madeira and reduce to a syrup, 6 to 8 minutes, then transfer to a small bowl. Cut the livers into halves or quarters and add to the large bowl with the chicken breast and mushrooms. Cover and refrigerate.

3. Put the ground pork in a food processor fitted with the steel blade, add the Madeira reduction and egg, and pulse until smooth, then season with salt and pepper. Transfer to a large bowl and stir in the cream. Cook a tablespoon of the mixture in a small pan, taste, and adjust the seasoning as necessary. Fold the chicken breast, livers, and mushrooms into the pork mixture.

4. When the dough is cool enough to handle, weigh out four 6-ounce/170-gram pieces and four 2-ounce/60-gram pieces. Shape the larger pieces into disks about the size of your pie dolly or mold, about 3 by ½ inch/7.5 by 1.25 centimeters. Press the smaller pieces into lids ⅛ to ¼ inch thick and the diameter of your pie dolly or mold. Refrigerate the pieces until they're cool and stiff but not solid, about 15 minutes. If the dough is too warm, it will not hold the shape of the pie dolly.

(recipe continues)

5. Begin shaping the larger disks into cups the size of your pie dolly or mold. The dough should be pliable and shouldn't crack as your hands warm it. Flour a pie dolly or mold and add some flour to the center of the first piece of dough so that the bottom of the pie dolly doesn't stick to the dough, then press the dolly into the center of the dough. Using your fingers, and with your thumbs on the top of the dolly, press the dough up around the dolly. Bring the dough about 3 inches/7.5 centimeters up the sides, checking regularly that the dolly isn't sticking to the dough. Transfer the dough, a 3-inch/7.5-centimeter cup, to a rimmed baking sheet and refrigerate it while you shape and chill the remaining three large pieces.

6. Preheat the oven to 375°F/190°C.

7. Remove the chilled dough cups from the fridge. Fill them almost all the way to the top with the meat mixture.

8. Press the smaller dough pieces into disks to fit the bottoms as lids, making a little ridge around the edges to prepare them for crimping. Moisten the edges of one lid and pinch it all around the cup to seal it. Do the same for the remaining lids.

9. Lightly brush the tops with egg wash, being careful not to let it pool. Crimp the edges of each pie using the three-finger method (see page 30), or crimp as desired. Use a knife or scissors to cut slits in the pie lids. Refrigerate for at least 15 minutes (or as long as overnight), then egg wash a second time.

10. Bake the pies until the internal temperature reaches 150°F/65°C, 45 to 60 minutes. Allow to rest for at least 15 minutes before serving.

SERVES 4

Here is a classic hand-raised pie, but Brian enlivens the interior with chunks of seared chicken and seared chicken liver for a nontraditional pie. When you're making the crusts for these pies, try to get the dough as thin as possible.

Chicken and Ham Hand-Raised Pies

These pies use a chicken and bacon filling, suspending within it chunks of ham. Use trim meat from chicken and mostly dark meat if you can. If it's all leg meat, be careful to remove all connective tissue. Feel free to ask your butcher to grind the bacon and chicken together for you. Or, if ground turkey is readily available, that can be substituted for the chicken, but the bacon still needs to be ground or very finely chopped.

14 ounces/400 grams boneless, skinless chicken, preferably mostly dark meat
8 ounces/225 grams smoked bacon
8 ounces/225 grams smoked ham, cut into medium dice
1 large egg, beaten
1 tablespoon minced garlic
2 tablespoons chopped fresh tarragon
2 tablespoons chopped fresh flat-leaf parsley
Kosher salt and freshly ground black pepper to taste
2 pounds/920 grams Hot-Water Dough (page 70), freshly made and allowed to cool slightly
Egg Wash (page 28)

1. Grind the chicken and bacon through a $\frac{3}{16}$-inch/5-millimeter or smaller die. Put it in a large bowl and add the ham, egg, garlic, tarragon, and parsley. Mix well and season with salt and pepper. Cook a tablespoon of the mixture in a small pan, taste, and adjust the seasoning as necessary. Cover the mixture and refrigerate it.

2. When the dough is cool enough to handle, weigh out four 6-ounce/170-gram pieces and four 2-ounce/60-gram pieces. Shape the larger pieces into disks about the size of your pie dolly or mold, about 3 by ½ inch/7.5 by 1.25 centimeters. Press the smaller pieces into lids ⅛ to ¼ inch thick and the diameter of your pie dolly or mold. Refrigerate the pieces until they're cool and stiff but not solid, about 15 minutes. If the dough is too warm, it will not hold the shape of the pie dolly.

3. Begin shaping the larger disks into cups the size of your pie dolly or mold. The dough should be pliable and shouldn't crack as your hands warm it. Flour a pie dolly or mold and add some flour to the center of the first piece of dough so that the bottom of the pie dolly doesn't stick to the dough, then press the dolly into the center of the dough. Using your fingers, and with your thumbs on the top of the dolly, press the dough up around the dolly. Bring the dough about 3 inches/7.5 centimeters up the sides, checking regularly that the dolly isn't sticking to the dough. Transfer the dough, a 3-inch/7.5-centimeter cup, to a rimmed baking sheet and refrigerate it while you shape and chill the remaining three large pieces.

4. Preheat the oven to 375°F/190°C.

5. Remove the chilled dough cups from the fridge. Fill them almost all the way to the top with the chilled meat mixture.

6. Press the smaller dough pieces into disks to fit the bottoms as lids, making a little ridge around the edges to prepare them for crimping. Moisten the edges of one lid and pinch it all around the cup to seal it. Do the same for the remaining lids.

7. Lightly brush the tops with egg wash, being careful not to let it pool. Crimp the edges of each pie using the three-finger method (see page 30), or crimp as desired. Use a knife or scissors to cut slits in the pie lids. Refrigerate for at least 15 minutes (or as long as overnight), then egg wash a second time.

8. Bake the pies until the internal temperature reaches 150°F/65°C, 45 to 60 minutes. Allow to rest for at least 15 minutes before serving.

SERVES 4

ROLLED RAISED PIES

Lamb Loin en Croûte with Spinach and
Pine Nuts   85

Mediterranean Vegetable Pie   88

Poached Salmon and Dill Rolled Pie   93

Salmon Rolled Pie with Shrimp and Spinach
Mousseline   96

Pork Tenderloin with Root Vegetables and
Mushrooms in Puff Pastry   98

Country Sausage Roll   99

Cumberland-Style Sausage Rolls   100

Cumberland-Style Sausage Rolls (page 100).

A rolled raised pie is one in which dough is wrapped around meat, fish, or vegetables, baked, and sliced to serve. Beef Wellington is a form of the rolled raised pie. It's among the easiest of the pies to make, as virtually anything can be wrapped in dough and baked with delicious results. It's not unlike making a strudel. And the Mediterranean Vegetable Pie (page 88) even looks strudel-like as we use a braided crust on top. The rolled raised pie is elegant in appearance and the dough-to-filling ratio always perfect.

The form is versatile. A couple of these recipes use whole loins of meat, but the filling doesn't necessarily have to be whole. If a filling can hold its shape, it can be used to make a rolled raised pie. Any of the fillings for the hand-raised pies can also be used to make a rolled raised pie.

In this chapter we have a range of styles, from ground meat to whole lamb and pork loins and two different rolled raised pies featuring salmon—one in which the fish is cooked first, then flaked and bound with a sauce; the other using a whole fillet of salmon that is stuffed with a shrimp and spinach mousseline.

We like to use a richer dough for these pies, either pâte brisée (which has the most fat) or 3-2-1 pie dough. Not only are they more flavorful, they're also easy to work with when rolling them out and wrapping the filling.

These are great pies to make when you're entertaining, as they can be prepared in advance and simply baked. They extend the number of portions of meat, so it's also an economical choice if you're serving an expensive protein such as lamb. Moreover, these pies make for an impressive presentation. You can't go wrong with a rolled raised pie.

Lamb Loin en Croûte *with Spinach and Pine Nuts*

This elegant pie using boneless lamb loin is a great lesson in how converting a dish into a pie extends the expensive meat. This much lamb alone would barely serve 4 people, but as a pie it serves 6 comfortably. It uses the same technique as the pork tenderloin rolled raised pie (page 98).

Brian first came by this recipe because he ran restaurants in Michigan where the clientele is thrifty. He wanted to serve lamb and his customers expected to see it offered, but there was no way he could afford to put a double-cut lamb chop on the menu at a price his customers would pay.

So he figured out economical ways to serve it, such as making lamb sausage and serving it with braised lamb breast. Or he would use the expensive lamb loin, but spread a layer of seasoned ground pork and lamb trimmings on top to extend the protein without compromising the flavor. Instead of serving 10 ounces/285 grams of lamb in the form of a double-cut chop, he served 4 ounces/115 grams; wrapped in a rich pastry and supplemented with the ground pork, it gave the same satisfaction.

In this recipe we use crêpes to serve as a barrier to protect the pastry from the meat juices.

2 (9-ounce/255-gram) boneless lamb loins, trimmed of all fat and sinew
  Kosher salt and freshly ground black pepper to taste
2 tablespoons vegetable oil
10 ounces/285 grams ground pork
¾ cup/85 grams tightly packed spinach leaves
1 tablespoon minced garlic
1 tablespoon minced shallot
1 tablespoon Dijon mustard
1 large egg white
3 tablespoons toasted pine nuts

12 ounces/340 grams Blitz Puff Pastry Dough (page 36) or 2 sheets store-bought puff pastry, thawed in the refrigerator
4 (8-inch/20-centimeter) Crêpes (page 27)
  Egg Wash (page 28)

1. Season the lamb loins all over with salt and pepper. Heat the oil in a large skillet over high heat. When the oil is hot, sear the lamb loins on all sides, leaving the centers raw, 3 to 4 minutes. Set aside to cool.

2. In a food processor, combine the pork, spinach, garlic, shallot, Dijon, egg white, salt, and pepper and puree until smooth. Fold in the pine nuts.

3. Pat the lamb loins dry with paper towels. Spread about one-quarter of the meat mixture over the top of each loin.

4. Roll out the puff pastry to an 8 by 20-inch/20 by 50-centimeter rectangle, then cut it in half width-wise to make two 8 by 10-inch/20 by 25-centimeter pieces and place on a sheet of parchment paper. Place a crêpe on each dough half. Place a lamb loin on each crêpe with the meat mixture side facing down. Spread the remaining meat mixture over the lamb loins so that they are fully encased. Place another crêpe on top of the meat.

5. For each pie, trim the pastry to the length of the coated loin. Roll the dough around the loin and cut the pastry to a 1-inch/2.5-centimeter overlap. Egg wash the overlap to seal the dough, leaving the ends exposed, then egg wash the entire top of the pastry. Carefully transfer the parchment and pies to a rimmed baking sheet and refrigerate for 15 minutes, then egg wash again.

6. Preheat the oven to 375°F/190°C.

7. Bake to an internal temperature of 125°F/50°C, 15 to 20 minutes. Let rest for 15 minutes before cutting.

SERVES 6

① These crêpes are very thin and loaded with chopped parsley.

② A crêpe has been trimmed to the length of the lamb loin coated in a spinach and pork forcemeat and will be rolled around the lamb. This will prevent juices from the spinach forcemeat from making the dough soggy.

③ Cut the dough to the length of the lamb loin and roll the lamb loin in it. Notice that the end has been egg washed to seal it.

④ A very good horsehair brush applies egg wash perfectly smoothly. This rolled pie will be refrigerated; when the egg wash is dry, it will get another coat.

Like a beef Wellington, this is an impressive dish, one that extends an expensive cut of lamb—and it's completely doable in the home kitchen. A forcemeat of pureed pork and spinach, with pine nuts folded in, is spread over a lamb loin, wrapped in a crêpe moisture barrier, then wrapped in puff pastry. Double egg washing gives it that gorgeous golden-brown exterior.

Mediterranean Vegetable Pie

This is a terrific vegetarian pie, filled with eggplant, zucchini, tomatoes, and onions, and enriched with goat cheese. It makes an excellent side dish but can also serve as a main course, thanks to the tasty, crispy dough surrounding the roasted vegetables.

While developing this pie in the classroom, Brian was having a little trouble with the bottom. There were so many vegetables releasing so much liquid that the bottom was not getting crisp. One day a colleague, Chef Jeff Gabriel, was walking by. Knowing that Jeff tries to keep fairly vegetarian, Brian showed him this pie and noted the problem. Immediately Jeff said, "Add some couscous" and walked off. So next time Brian's class made this pie, Brian instructed them to sprinkle a thin layer of dried Moroccan couscous between some of the layers as they built them up. It worked brilliantly, the couscous absorbing the liquid released by the vegetables, and illustrated one of the many reasons Brian loves working with such knowledgeable chefs and how important it is to share information with other culinarians.

This pie uses an interesting braided dough technique (see page 90), which is not only aesthetically pleasing but also practical in that the gaps in the dough allow the copious moisture to escape during baking so that the dough remains crisp.

1 large eggplant, sliced crosswise ½ inch/1.25 centimeters thick (about 8 slices)
2 zucchinis, sliced crosswise ¼ inch/6 millimeters thick (about 20 slices)
3 Roma tomatoes, halved lengthwise
¼ cup/60 milliliters olive oil
　 Kosher salt and freshly ground black pepper to taste
1 large yellow or red bell pepper
1 tablespoon vegetable oil
1 cup/130 grams julienne of sweet onion
12 ounces/340 grams Blitz Puff Pastry Dough (page 36) or 2 sheets store-bought puff pastry, thawed in the refrigerator
¼ cup/40 grams uncooked Moroccan couscous
4 ounces/115 grams goat cheese
10 large fresh basil leaves
　 Egg Wash (page 28)

1. Preheat the oven to 400°F/205°C.

2. Spread out the eggplant, zucchini, and tomato halves in a single layer on a rimmed baking sheet. Drizzle all over with the olive oil and season heavily with salt and pepper. Roast until soft and slightly brown around the edges, 20 to 25 minutes. Cool completely.

3. Roast the bell pepper over an open flame until the skin turns black and blisters. (Alternatively, you can cut the pepper in half and broil until blackened.) Put the pepper in a bowl and cover tightly with plastic wrap. When cool, remove the charred skin and seeds. Cut lengthwise into 6 strips.

4. Heat the vegetable oil in a large sauté pan over medium heat. When the oil is hot, add the onion and sauté until tender but not browned, 5 to 10 minutes. Transfer to a plate to cool.

5. Roll out the puff pastry to an 8 by 20-inch/20 by 50-centimeter rectangle. Place it on a sheet of parchment paper.

6. Make a series of diagonal slices on each long side of the dough: First, cut 2 inches/5 centimeters off the top two corners of the rectangle at a 45-degree angle. Measure 2½ inches/6 centimeters in from each long side and draw a line the length of the pastry, leaving a 3-inch/7.5-centimeter strip down the center of the dough where the vegetables will be placed. Following the 45-degree angle cut from the corners, make 15 angled cuts ½ inch/1.25 centimeters wide all the way down. At the bottom, cut the small triangle out that forms the last strip at the 2½-inch/6-centimeter mark. The idea is to create strips that you will fold over the vegetables, alternately, creating a braided pattern.

7. In the center part of the pastry, shingle the eggplant slices, then dust them with couscous. Spread the cooked onion on the eggplant, then shingle the zucchini slices over the onion Sprinkle with more couscous. Top the zucchini with a layer of goat cheese. Top the goat cheese with the roasted pepper strips. Dust with the remaining couscous. Lay the basil leaves down the center and finish with the tomatoes, cut sides down.

8. Fold the pastry strips over the vegetables, alternating sides to give a braided look. Carefully transfer the parchment and pie to a rimmed baking sheet.

9. Egg wash the dough, refrigerate for 15 minutes, then egg wash again.

10. Bake until the crust is golden brown and the vegetables are hot, 35 to 40 minutes. Cool slightly before cutting.

SERVES 6 (OR 8 TO 10 AS AN APPETIZER)

① Vegetables and goat cheese are layered on the dough. The sides have been cut at 45-degree angles so that they will form a braid over the vegetables. Importantly, each layer has been "dusted" with Moroccan couscous, which will absorb the excess moisture and keep the crust crisp.

② Fold the dough strips over the vegetables, alternating left and right.

③ Egg wash the entire pie. Notice how uneven, even sloppy, the pie looks at this stage, and compare it with the finished pie.

④ The finished Mediterranean Vegetable Pie.

Poached Salmon and Dill Rolled Pie

In the professional kitchen, there is always trim from protein to use, and chefs are forever figuring out ways to avoid wasting any fresh ingredient. This pie is a result of just that, when Brian had a lot of salmon left over from trimming fillets, mostly tail and belly, at the restaurant. It's great to use trim to make this pie if you have it (perhaps left over from making the Salmon Rolled Pie with Shrimp and Spinach Mousseline on page 96), but whole fillets work beautifully as well. This pie requires a moisture barrier in the form of crêpes, which help hold the filling in place and facilitate the crust getting crisp. Make sure the sauce that binds the flaked salmon is thick enough or it can weep out when the rolled raised pie is cut.

The instructions below are for shaping the pie into a log. For a decorative fish shape, see pages 94–95.

½ cup/120 millimeters fish or chicken stock
12 ounces/340 grams boneless, skinless salmon (ideally trim from the belly and tail)
¼ cup/60 milliliters heavy cream
2 tablespoons beurre manié (see page 46), or as needed
2 tablespoons unsalted butter
1 cup/80 grams thinly sliced onion
½ cup/30 grams sliced button mushrooms
3 tablespoons drained capers
½ cup/30 grams fresh dill leaves, finely chopped
Kosher salt and freshly ground black pepper to taste
12 ounces/340 grams Pâte Brisée (page 33)
2 (8-inch/20-centimeter) Crêpes (page 27)
3 large hard-cooked eggs, peeled and sliced
Egg Wash (page 28)

1. In a shallow sauté pan, bring the stock to a bare simmer over medium-high heat. Add the salmon and poach it until it's just cooked but still moist and flaky, about 5 minutes. Using a slotted spoon or tongs, transfer the salmon to a bowl to cool. Add the cream to the cooking liquid, bring it to a simmer, and reduce it by one-quarter, about 10 minutes. Whisk in the beurre manié to thicken the sauce to a gravy-like consistency. Remove the pan from the heat.

2. Melt the butter in a large sauté pan over medium heat. Add the onion and gently cook until soft, 3 to 4 minutes. Add the mushrooms and cook until soft, another 5 minutes or so. Remove the pan from the heat.

3. Gently flake the fish. Add the onion mixture to the fish, along with the capers and dill. Season with salt and pepper. Add just enough of the sauce to bind all the ingredients together. Cover and chill the mixture.

4. Preheat the oven to 400°F/205°C. Line a rimmed baking sheet with parchment paper.

5. Roll out the dough to a 14 by 8-inch/35 by 20-centimeter rectangle. Lay the crêpes on the dough, slightly overlapping so that they cover the dough. Shingle the egg slices on the crêpes, two slices of egg side by side, down the center of the crêpes. Spread the salmon mixture over the eggs, down the center.

6. Egg wash one long edge of the dough. Fold the crêpes and dough over the salmon, creating a log with the seam on top. Roll the log over onto the lined baking sheet, seam side down. Tuck the ends of the dough underneath so that the salmon is enclosed. Egg wash the dough, refrigerate for 15 minutes, then egg wash again. With scissors, snip several vent holes along the top.

7. Bake until golden brown, 35 to 40 minutes. Allow to rest for 15 minutes before cutting.

SERVES 4

① While the recipe instructs you to make this pie in the shape of a log, it's easy to make decorative pies, especially for fish. Cut out two pieces in the simple shape of a fish. Cut out a decorative crescent shape, to represent the gill, preferably with a fluted pastry wheel. Reserve a small ball of dough for the eye. Mold the cooked filling of salmon and dill in the center.

② Egg wash the edge of the bottom piece of dough and cover the filling with the second piece of dough. Press to seal. Crimp the edge up to the mouth with the tines of a fork or, if you have one, a crimper like the one shown here. Egg wash the pie.

③ Place the eye and the gill on the egg-washed dough. Using a small ring cutter or paring knife, cut decorative scales.

④ The finished pies. (Note: The recipe for the rolled version of this pie calls for a crêpe barrier and hard-cooked egg, shingled down the center of the dough; for the decorative pie, the egg has been roughly chopped and folded into the filling; no egg barrier is used for the decorative pies. The decorative pies will take less time to cook, 25 to 30 minutes; both pies should be cooked until golden brown and hot inside.)

Salmon Rolled Pie
with Shrimp and Spinach Mousseline

For this pie, a salmon fillet is stuffed with a shrimp and spinach mousseline. It would be elegant on its own, but by baking it in a rich crust it becomes a beautiful centerpiece of a meal. It's also a very easy, straightforward preparation. The salmon fillet is butterflied, the interior is spread with the mousseline, which is then enclosed within the salmon, which in turn is wrapped in pie dough. This works best if you start with a rectangular piece of fish. Buy a whole fillet and trim the belly and tail, leaving the thickest part for this recipe. The trim can be used for the Poached Salmon and Dill Rolled Pie (page 93).

Note that the shrimp will be pureed, so don't splurge on big individual shrimp. Save those for a shrimp cocktail and buy smaller, less expensive shrimp for this recipe.

- 1 (2-pound/900-gram) boneless, skinless salmon fillet
  Kosher salt and freshly ground black pepper to taste
- 4 ounces/115 grams shrimp, peeled and deveined
- 1 large egg white
- ¾ cup/85 grams fresh spinach leaves
- ½ cup/120 milliliters heavy cream
- 1 pound/450 grams 3-2-1 Pie Dough (page 33)
  Egg Wash (page 28)

1. Butterfly the salmon fillet lengthwise, and open like a book. Season it with salt and pepper.

2. In a food processor, puree the shrimp with the egg white, salt, and pepper. Add the spinach and, while running the processor, slowly add the cream. The mixture should be a nice light green. Cook a small spoonful in barely simmering water until heated through, 5 minutes or so, then taste; add more salt and pepper if you wish and pulse again.

3. Preheat the oven to 375°F/190°C. Line a rimmed baking sheet with parchment paper.

4. Roll out the dough to a 16 by 10-inch/40 by 25-centimeter rectangle.

5. Spread the shrimp mixture down the length of the salmon, then fold the salmon over the filling, completely encasing the shrimp mousse in the salmon.

6. Place the salmon in the middle of the dough. Egg wash the edges to be sealed. Fold the two long ends over the fish, overlapping by about ¾ inch/2 centimeters. Roll it over onto the lined baking sheet, seam side down. Tuck the dough ends under to fully enclose the salmon. Egg wash the top, refrigerate for 15 minutes, then egg wash again. With scissors, snip vent holes along the top.

7. Bake until golden brown and the internal temperature is 135°F/57°C, 20 to 25 minutes. Allow it to rest for 15 minutes before cutting.

SERVES 6

This pie begins with a raw fillet of salmon, which is butterflied and filled with a shrimp and spinach mousseline, then encased in dough and baked. Be careful not to overcook the fish—it should just hit 135°F/57°C. This fish is cooked perfectly—moist and just opaque. It's served here with Sweet Onion Sauce (page 195).

Pork Tenderloin
with Root Vegetables and Mushrooms in Puff Pastry

This recipe is very much in the style of beef Wellington, but it uses a pork tenderloin instead of beef, and rather than being spread with mushroom duxelles, the pork is spread with a puree of ground pork loaded with sautéed root vegetables. The fatty ground pork adds succulence and flavor to the lean tenderloin. The meat is first wrapped in a crêpe to prevent any juices from reaching the buttery puff pastry, keeping the interior moist while allowing the pastry to stay crisp. (The finished pie is pictured on page 201.)

1 (12-ounce/360-gram) pork tenderloin,
   trimmed of all fat and sinew
   Kosher salt and freshly ground black pepper
   to taste
2 to 4 tablespoons vegetable oil
¼ cup/25 grams small-diced carrots
¼ cup/25 grams small-diced parsnips
1 tablespoon minced garlic
1 tablespoon minced shallot
½ cup/30 grams quartered small button
   mushrooms
3 tablespoons Madeira wine
2 tablespoons finely chopped soft fresh herbs
   (such as flat-leaf parsley, chives, and/or
   tarragon)
8 ounces/225 grams fatty pork shoulder, finely
   ground
1 large egg
2 (8-inch/20-centimeter) Crêpes (page 27)
8 ounces/225 grams Blitz Puff Pastry Dough
   (page 36) or 1 sheet store-bought puff pastry,
   thawed in the refrigerator
   Egg Wash (page 28)

1. Season the tenderloin with salt and pepper. Heat 2 tablespoons oil in a large, heavy-bottomed sauté pan over medium-high heat. When the oil is hot, sear the tenderloin on all sides, browning it nicely while leaving the center raw, 3 to 4 minutes. Transfer to a plate to cool.

2. In the same pan (adding more oil if necessary), sauté the carrots, parsnips, garlic, and shallot over medium heat until the carrots and parsnips are tender, 7 to 8 minutes. Add the mushrooms and cook until tender but without browning anything, 5 to 7 minutes. Add the Madeira and reduce until almost dry, 7 to 8 minutes. Set aside to cool completely. Add the chopped herbs.

3. In a food processor, puree the ground pork with the egg, ½ teaspoon salt, and pepper to taste, just until smooth. Transfer the mixture to a large bowl and fold in the sautéed vegetables. Cook a tablespoon of the mixture in a small pan, taste, and adjust the seasoning as necessary.

4. Pat the pork tenderloin dry with paper towels. Using a pallet knife or small offset spatula, spread about half of the vegetable mixture evenly on one side of the tenderloin. Flip the tenderloin over onto a crêpe, vegetable side down. Spread the remaining vegetable mixture on top, creating an even layer all the way around the tenderloin. Trim the second crêpe so the entire tenderloin (except the ends) is covered by the crêpes.

5. Preheat the oven to 375°F/190°C. Line a rimmed baking sheet with parchment paper.

6. Roll the dough into an 8 by 10-inch/20 by 25-centimeter rectangle. Lay the wrapped pork tenderloin in the center. Egg wash one edge of the dough and roll it into a log, leaving the ends open and unsealed. Place the log on the lined baking sheet, seam side down. Egg wash the top, refrigerate for 15 minutes, and egg wash a second time.

7. Bake to an internal temperature of 140°F/60°C, 30 to 45 minutes. Allow it to rest for 15 minutes before cutting.

SERVES 4

Country Sausage Roll

We call this a "country" sausage roll because it's rustic—like a pâté grandmère. The forcemeat is seasoned with salt and pepper, fresh herbs, roasted garlic, nutmeg, and cayenne, and loaded with sweet-savory sautéed onion and mushrooms and diced ham.

The recipe calls for cooking the sausage roll entirely raw. If you prefer, however, another method is to cook and cool the sausage first, then wrap it in dough and bake it. This method involves an extra step but results in a more uniform sausage roll (when cooked from raw, the meat expands during cooking, then contracts, leaving gaps between the meat and the crust). If you would like to try the alternative method, roll the sausage (pork and all the seasonings) in oiled aluminum foil rather than plastic wrap and bake it on a rimmed baking sheet at 375°F/190°C until it reaches an internal temperature of 140°F/60°C, about 30 minutes. Let it cool, then chill it completely and proceed with placing it on the dough as in the main recipe.

- 3 tablespoons vegetable oil
- ½ cup/40 grams quartered mushrooms
- ½ cup/90 grams small-diced onion
- 1 pound/450 grams coarsely ground pork
- 6 ounces/170 grams medium-diced Canadian bacon or ham
- 2 tablespoons roasted garlic (see page 71)
- 2 tablespoons chopped fresh marjoram
- 2 tablespoons chopped fresh flat-leaf parsley
- 1 large egg
- 1 tablespoon kosher salt
- 1 teaspoon freshly ground black pepper
- ½ teaspoon grated fresh nutmeg
- ¼ teaspoon cayenne pepper
- 8 ounces/225 grams Pâte Brisée (page 33)
  Egg Wash (page 28)

1. Heat 2 tablespoons oil in a large sauté pan over high heat. When the oil is smoking hot, add the mushrooms in one layer and press down hard to sear them before they begin to drop their liquid. When they are tender, after a minute or two, transfer to a plate.

2. Wipe out the pan, add the remaining 1 tablespoon oil, and sauté the onion until translucent and just beginning to brown, 2 to 3 minutes. Transfer to the plate with the mushrooms and let cool.

3. In a large bowl, combine the pork, bacon, roasted garlic, marjoram, parsley, egg, salt, black pepper, nutmeg, and cayenne and mix well. Cook a tablespoons of the mixture in a small pan, taste, and adjust the seasoning as necessary. Fold in the cooled mushrooms and onion.

4. Lay a 14-inch/35-centimeter length of plastic wrap on a work surface. Spread the meat mixture out into a log on the plastic and roll it up, twisting the ends. It should come out to a log that is 9 inches/23 centimeters long and 2 inches/5 centimeters in diameter. Chill completely.

5. Preheat the oven to 375°F/190°C. Line a rimmed baking sheet with parchment paper.

6. Roll out the dough to an 8 by 10-inch/20 by 25-centimeter rectangle. Unwrap the meat and place it in the middle of the dough. (If you have precooked the sausage, remove it from the fridge, unwrap it, and proceed from here.) Egg wash one edge of the dough. Roll the dough around the meat and place on the lined baking sheet, seam side down. Egg wash the roll, refrigerate it for 15 minutes, then egg wash it again. Use scissors to snip 8 to 10 vent holes in the top.

7. Bake until the center reaches an internal temperature of 140°F/60°C, 15 to 20 minutes (if you have precooked your pork, there's no need to measure the temperature here as it's already cooked). Allow the sausage roll to rest for 15 minutes before cutting.

SERVES 4

Cumberland-Style Sausage Rolls

This sausage recipe dates back some 500 years. It has protected geographical indication status, which means that in order for a sausage to be called Cumberland, it must be made in Cumberland County, England; this is why we use the term "Cumberland-style" here. Wrapping the sausage in dough takes the humble sausage to a different level. The crisp crust adds to the eating experience of this highly seasoned, peppery-nutmeggy sausage.

If you don't want to make your own Cumberland sausage using the recipe below, you can use eight 4-ounce/115-gram store-bought sausages. Simply wrap them in dough and bake. Serve these with a nice whole-grain mustard.

    3 pounds/1360 grams pork shoulder
 1⅓ cups/150 grams dry bread crumbs
 1½ tablespoons kosher salt
    1 tablespoon rubbed sage
    1 tablespoon freshly ground black pepper
    1 teaspoon ground white pepper
    1 teaspoon grated fresh nutmeg
  ½ teaspoon ground mace
  ¼ teaspoon dried marjoram
  ⅛ teaspoon cayenne pepper
  ¼ cup/60 milliliters water
    6 feet/1.8 meters hog casing, rinsed
    2 pounds/900 grams Pâte Brisée (page 33)
        Egg Wash (page 28)
        Sesame or poppy seeds, for sprinkling

1. Combine the pork, bread crumbs, salt, sage, black pepper, white pepper, nutmeg, mace, marjoram, and cayenne in a large bowl. Grind the mixture through a ⅜-inch/9-millimeter die into another large bowl. Add the water and mix by hand until sticky. Cook a tablespoon in a small pan, taste, and adjust the seasoning as necessary.

2. Stuff the mixture into the hog casing and tie off or link into 8 even sausages. Chill.

3. Bring a large pot of water to 180°F/82°C. Add the sausages, making sure they are completely submerged, and poach until the sausages are firm to the touch but not hard, 20 to 25 minutes. Drain and chill.

4. Cut the dough in half and roll out each into a 10 by 12-inch/25 by 30-centimeter rectangle. Cut 8 strips from each rectangle, for a total of 16 strips, that are 12 inches/30 centimeters long and about 1¼ inches/3 centimeters wide.

5. Line a rimmed baking sheet with parchment paper. Pat the sausages dry with paper towels. To wrap each sausage, start at one end and wrap a strip of dough in a spiral around the bottom half of the sausage. Repeat with another strip of dough to wrap the top half. Place on the lined baking sheet and chill.

6. Preheat the oven to 375°F/190°C.

7. Egg wash the top of each wrapped sausage, refrigerate for 15 minutes, then egg wash again. Sprinkle with sesame or poppy seeds.

8. Bake until the crust is golden brown and the sausage is hot all the way through, 20 to 25 minutes.

SERVES 8

Two different types of sausage rolls are featured here. The larger one is filled with a **country sausage** (page 99), using loose sausage shaped into a log and wrapped in dough (foreground on the plate, sliced from the roll immediately behind the plate). The smaller slices are individual **Cumberland-style sausages** with strips of dough wrapped around a sausage link. Here, we serve them with Faux French's Mustard (page 191) and Quick-Pickled Red Cabbage (page 184).

THE SAVORY PIES

TARTS AND GALETTES

German Heirloom Cottage Cheese Pie   105

Five-Onion Pie   106

Hot-Smoked Salmon and Dill Pie   108

Leek Gratin Pie   109

Leek and Potato Pie   111

Smoked Atlantic Haddock Pie   112

Spanish Chorizo, Goat Cheese, and
   Red Pepper Pie   115

Spinach and Mushroom Galette   116

Stilton Cheesecake with Walnut Crust   119

Summer Tomato Tart   120

Sweet Potato Galette   122

The Best Mushroom Tart   125

Spanish Chorizo, Goat Cheese, and Red Pepper Pie (page 115).

Single-crust pies with the crust on the bottom, more commonly referred to as tarts, are among the easiest and most forgiving of the pies. A tart is made in some kind of mold (we use a 10-inch/25-centimeter fluted tart pan with a removable bottom). *Galette* is the term we use for a freeform crust, probably the easiest type of pie in the canon: Dough is rolled into a disk and topped with the main ingredient or ingredients, then the edges are folded up to form a rim.

These single-crust pies seem to lend themselves to vegetarian preparations; virtually all of the dozen pies in this chapter are either vegetarian or pescatarian. For meat eaters, we highly recommend the Spanish Chorizo, Goat Cheese, and Red Pepper Pie (page 115).

The German Heirloom Cottage Cheese Pie (page 105) is the only pie in this book that's on the sweeter side, and it uses an excellent sour cream crust. All of the other pies in this chapter use either the 3-2-1 Pie Dough (page 33) or the richer Pâte Brisée (page 33)—either will work, if you prefer one over the other. Tarts and galettes have the highest crust-to-filling ratio, which means that a delicious crust is a significant part of the dish. For that reason we really do recommend making your own dough with real butter.

German Heirloom Cottage Cheese Pie

Brian picked up this preparation from a colleague, Jeff Gabriel, who teaches in Schoolcraft's baking program. It uses a sour cream pastry dough that results in a very tender crust. The rich, creamy filling is on the sweeter side and heavily flavored with lemon zest. It makes a great brunch item, served with any kind of fruit compote. Be sure to use the best cottage cheese available, one that's at least 4 percent fat.

- 1 pound/450 grams cottage cheese (at least 4% fat)
- 2 large eggs, beaten
  Grated zest and juice of 1 lemon
- ¼ cup/60 milliliters heavy cream
- 2 teaspoons vanilla extract
- ¼ cup/50 grams granulated sugar
- 2 tablespoons all-purpose flour
- 2 teaspoons kosher salt
- 10 ounces/285 grams Sour Cream Pastry Dough (recipe follows), blind baked in a 10-inch/25-centimeter tart pan (see page 25)

1. Preheat the oven to 375°F/190°C.

2. In a standing mixer fitted with the paddle attachment, combine all the ingredients (except the tart shell!) and mix until combined. This can be done in a large bowl with a sturdy whisk as well.

3. Pour the batter into the blind-baked tart shell and bake it until it's set, 35 to 40 minutes. Cool before cutting.

SERVES 8

Sour Cream Pastry Dough

- 5 ounces/140 grams chilled unsalted butter, cut into ¼-inch/6-millimeter dice
- 9 ounces/270 grams (about 3½ cups) all-purpose flour
- ½ teaspoon/3 grams kosher salt
- ¾ cup/150 grams cold sour cream
- 2 tablespoons ice-cold water

1. In a large bowl, combine the butter, flour, and salt. With your hands, press the flour into the butter until the mixture resembles very coarse meal but is not quite cornmeal-looking.

2. Add the sour cream and, with a fork or pastry cutter, combine until a paste forms. Add the ice water a little at a time until the mixture forms a dough. Do not overwork the dough or it will become tough.

3. Divide the dough in half and wrap in plastic wrap. If using that day, refrigerate for at least 30 minutes before rolling it out. If you won't be using it that day or next, freeze for up to 3 weeks.

YIELD: 1¼ POUNDS/570 GRAMS DOUGH (enough for two 10-inch/25-centimeter tarts)

Five-Onion Pie

This is like a simplified Alsatian tart. Various kinds of onions are sautéed, then combined with a small amount of custard, poured into a shell, and baked. It's a perfect side to beef or pork but would go equally well with a salad. It's even great for breakfast with a fried or poached egg on top. Serve hot, cold, or at room temperature.

4 ounces/115 grams unsalted butter

¾ cup/150 grams short, fine julienne of Spanish onion

¾ cup/150 grams short, fine julienne of red onion

¾ cup/150 grams sliced leek whites (cut crosswise into ½-inch/1.25-centimer pieces)

½ cup/90 grams fine julienne of shallots

150 grams sliced scallion whites and greens, reserved separately (5 or 6 scallions)
 Kosher salt and freshly ground black pepper to taste

1 large egg

¾ cup/180 milliliters heavy cream

12 ounces/340 grams Pâte Brisée (page 33), blind baked in a 10-inch/25-centimeter tart pan (see page 25)

3 ounces/85 grams grated Parmigiano-Reggiano or pecorino cheese

1. Preheat the oven to 375°F/190°C.

2. Melt the butter in a large, heavy-bottomed sauté pan over medium heat. Add the Spanish onion, red onion, leek whites, shallots, and scallion whites, season with salt and pepper, cover, and cook until soft, 3 to 4 minutes. Uncover and turn the heat to high to allow any excess liquid to cook off. Remove the pan from the heat and cool to room temperature.

3. In a large bowl, whisk together the egg and cream until they're uniformly combined, then stir in the cooled onions and scallion greens. Pour into the blind-baked tart shell and scatter the cheese evenly over the onion custard.

4. Bake until cheese is browned and the filling is set, 30 to 35 minutes. Cool completely before cutting.

SERVES 8

This **Five-Onion Pie** makes a great accompaniment to a main course or a lovely light meal with a salad. Notice how much dough overhang there is—this will be cut off with a serrated knife after the tart is filled and finished (like the Spanish Chorizo pictured on page 114). Were you to trim the crust before filling it, you'd risk cracking the interior crust. This tart is finished with freshly grated Parmigiano-Reggiano.

Hot-Smoked Salmon and Dill Pie

One of the most intriguing things about charcuterie is the innovative ways it teaches us to use trim and small pieces of an expensive product to create delicious, beautiful dishes from what had been scraps. Typically hot-smoked fish—that is, fish that's cooked while it's smoked, as opposed to cold-smoked salmon, which is not cooked—is cooked on the bone so that when you remove the larger pieces of meat, there will always be fragments of the meat that can be used. While this is especially important to chefs watching food costs, using all your trim at home shouldn't be taken for granted.

Again, this recipe uses cooked smoked salmon, not the kind of smoked salmon you put on your bagel, which is cured and smoked. This recipe will work with any cooked smoked fish—smoked trout, smoked sablefish, blue fish, or the king of smoked fish, sturgeon. We like to eat this pie hot, but some may love it cold. Like many of the tarts here, the main ingredient is bound by a custard and then baked.

12 ounces/335 grams hot-smoked salmon, flaked
 1 cup/120 grams minced red onion
 1 cup/60 grams thinly sliced scallions
 3 tablespoons chopped fresh dill leaves
 3 tablespoons capers, drained
 2 large eggs
 1 cup/240 milliliters heavy cream
    Kosher salt and freshly ground black pepper to taste
12 ounces/340 grams Pâte Brisée (page 33), blind baked in a 10-inch/25-centimeter tart pan (see page 25)

1. Preheat the oven to 350°F/175°C.

2. In a large bowl, combine the salmon, red onion, scallions, dill, and capers and toss to distribute the ingredients.

3. In a small bowl, whisk together the eggs and cream until uniformly combined, then season it with salt and pepper. Pour the eggs and cream over the fish mixture and fold the ingredients together. Pour the mixture into the blind-baked tart shell, spreading the mixture to fill the tart shell evenly.

4. Bake until set, 30 to 35 minutes. Allow the tart to rest for at least 15 minutes before cutting.

SERVES 6

Leek Gratin Pie

This is a great pie for onion lovers. The leeks get very sweet. It's less creamy than the Leek and Potato Pie (page 111), but the Gruyère cheese turns golden-brown and melty.

The leeks, an underused aromatic vegetable, are very forward here. Leeks vary widely in size, but this recipe requires 2 good-sized leeks, 1 to 1½ inches/2.5 to 3.25 centimeters in diameter. Remember that leeks are notorious for carrying dirt. After halving them, be sure to check them carefully for dirt as you wash them.

- 2 ounces/60 grams unsalted butter
- 2 large leeks (about 1 pound/450 grams), halved lengthwise, cleaned, and sliced crosswise into ¼-inch/6-millimeter pieces
  Kosher salt and freshly ground black pepper to taste
- ¾ cup/180 milliliters heavy cream
- 1 large egg, thoroughly whisked
- 12 ounces/340 grams Pâte Brisée (page 33), blind baked in a 10-inch/25-centimeter tart pan (see page 25)
- 3 ounces/90 grams Gruyère cheese, grated

1. Preheat the oven to 350°F/175°C.

2. Melt the butter in a large, heavy-bottomed sauté pan over medium heat. Add the leeks and season with salt and pepper. Cover and cook until tender but not browned, about 5 minutes. Uncover, turn the heat up to medium-high, and allow the moisture to cook off, stirring to prevent browning.

3. When the pan is almost dry, add the cream, bring it to a boil, and reduce by about half, until it's thick but not dry, 6 to 7 minutes. Remove from the heat and allow it to come to room temperature.

4. Stir in the egg.

5. Spread the creamed leeks in the blind-baked tart shell and top with the cheese.

6. Bake until the custard is set and the cheese has browned, about 20 minutes. Let it cool to room temperature before cutting.

SERVES 6 TO 8

Leek and Potato Pie

Leeks, potatoes, cream, and Gruyère cheese—it's hard to go wrong with this truly felicitous combination of ingredients. And the pie couldn't be easier to make: Leeks are cooked in cream to form the base, disks of cooked potato are shingled across the base, and then everything is covered with cheese. It's a delicious, rich pie, especially fine on a cold night.

- 2 pounds/900 grams russet potatoes
- 2 tablespoons unsalted butter
- 2 large leeks (about 1 pound/450 grams), halved lengthwise, cleaned, and sliced crosswise into ¼-inch/6-millimeter pieces
  Kosher salt and freshly ground black pepper to taste
- 1 cup/240 milliliters plus ⅓ cup/80 milliliters heavy cream
- 12 ounces/340 grams 3-2-1 Pie Dough (page 33), blind baked in a 10-inch/25-centimeter tart pan (see page 25)
- 3 ounces/90 grams Gruyère cheese, grated
- 2 ounces/60 grams Parmigiano-Reggiano cheese, grated

1. Put the potatoes in a medium pot, cover with cold water, and bring to a boil. Turn the heat down and simmer until soft when pierced with a skewer, 20 to 30 minutes. Drain and allow to cool.

2. Melt the butter in a large, heavy-bottomed sauté pan over medium heat. Add the leeks, season with salt and pepper, cover, and cook until tender, about 5 minutes. Uncover, turn the heat up to high, and add 1 cup/240 milliliters cream. Bring to a boil, then turn the heat down and simmer until the mixture is thick and creamy, about 5 minutes. Set aside to cool.

3. Preheat the oven to 350°F/175°C.

4. When the potatoes are cool enough to handle, peel them and slice into ¼-inch/6-millimeter-thick disks.

5. Spread the creamed leeks in the bottom of the blind-baked tart shell. Shingle the potatoes on top in a circle until the leeks are completely covered. Season the top with salt and pepper. Drizzle the remaining ⅓ cup/80 milliliters cream over the potatoes. Sprinkle both cheeses evenly over the top.

6. Bake until the top is browned and the pie is heated through, about 30 minutes. Allow to rest for 15 minutes before cutting.

SERVES 8

The inspiration for this pie came from Paula Wolfert's *The Cooking of Southwest France*, published 35 years ago. Brian has been making a version ever since. Southwest France is a land of hearty, rustic fare—think duck confit, cassoulet, and rich potato dishes like this **Leek and Potato Pie**. Notice the thick, crunchy layer of potato on top and the creamy leeks below. Served hot, this pie is deeply comforting to eat.

Smoked Atlantic Haddock Pie

At one time, haddock and cod were plentiful and inexpensive, so this would have been a common pie. The lean, white meat is sweet and the texture flaky. Brian loves New England chowder and used to make it with haddock instead of clams. Then he started smoking the fish and this pie came out of that—chowder in a crust. If you don't have a smoker or store-bought is not available, any smoked and cooked fish will work here.

- ¾ cup/100 grams small-diced russet potato
- 2 tablespoons unsalted butter
- 1 large leek (about 8 ounces/225 grams), white part only, halved lengthwise, cleaned, and thinly sliced
  Kosher salt and freshly ground black pepper to taste
- 4 ounces/112 grams button mushrooms, sliced
- 10 ounces/280 grams hot-smoked haddock, cleaned and flaked
- 2 tablespoons chopped fresh soft herbs (such as chives, tarragon, flat-leaf parsley, and/or chervil)
- 2 large eggs
- 1 cup/240 milliliters heavy whipping cream
- 12 ounces/340 grams Pâte Brisée (page 33), blind baked in a 10-inch/25-centimeter tart pan (see page 25)
- 2 ounces/56 grams grated white cheddar cheese

1. Preheat the oven to 350°F/175°C.

2. Put the potato in a small pot, cover with cold water, and bring to a boil. Turn the heat down and simmer just until tender, 10 to 15 minutes. Drain and set aside to cool.

3. Meanwhile, melt the butter in a large sauté pan over medium heat. Add the leek and season with salt and pepper. Cover and cook the leeks until tender, about 5 minutes. Uncover, add the mushrooms, and cook until most of the juices have evaporated, 7 to 8 minutes. Transfer the mixture to a large bowl and set aside to cool.

4. Add the haddock, potato, and herbs to the leek and mushrooms and toss gently to distribute the ingredients.

5. In a small bowl, whisk together the eggs and cream until they're uniformly combined. Season with salt and pepper, then fold into the haddock mixture.

6. Pour the mixture into the blind-baked tart shell. Sprinkle the cheese evenly over the top. Bake until set, 30 to 35 minutes.

SERVES 6 TO 8

This pie features smoked haddock with potatoes and leeks, but any hearty smoked fish will work. It's important to let this pie cool so that you can make clean slices. Once sliced, it should be reheated in a 350°F/175°C oven and served hot.

Spanish Chorizo, Goat Cheese, and Red Pepper Pie

Choosing the right chorizo makes a huge difference in the outcome of this pie. A variety of different regional chorizos are available, including fresh (raw) Mexican-style chorizo, but for this pie you want a dry-style sausage, but not hard like a salami. Though we've been making our own for years (see the recipe in *Charcuterie*), we wouldn't expect you to smoke and dry-cure a sausage for this recipe. Excellent Spanish chorizo is available from Whole Foods Market and online from La Tienda. It adds the right amount of flavor without overpowering the other ingredients and maintains a nice texture without being chewy.

- 2 tablespoons olive oil
- ½ cup/100 grams small-diced onion
- 2 red bell peppers, seeded and small-diced
- 10 ounces/285 grams dried Spanish chorizo, small-diced
- 3 large eggs
- 1½ cups/360 milliliters heavy cream
  Kosher salt and freshly ground black pepper to taste
- ¼ cup/14 grams thinly sliced scallions
- ¼ cup/14 grams coarsely chopped fresh cilantro
- 12 ounces/340 grams Pâte Brisée (page 33), blind-baked in a 10-inch/25-centimeter tart pan (see page 25)
- 9 ounces/255 grams goat cheese, at room temperature

1. Preheat the oven to 350°F/175°C.

2. Heat the olive oil in a large sauté pan over medium heat. When the oil is hot, add the onion, bell peppers, and chorizo and sauté until soft, 3 to 4 minutes. Set aside to cool.

3. In a large bowl, whisk together the eggs and cream until uniformly combined, then season with salt and pepper. Add the cooled onion, pepper, and chorizo to the egg mixture. Fold in the scallions and cilantro, then pour it all into the blind-baked tart shell. Dot the top of the pie with the softened goat cheese.

4. Bake just until set and not runny, 30 to 40 minutes. Allow to cool before cutting.

SERVES 8

This pie combines dry-cured Spanish chorizo, red bell pepper, onion, scallion, and cilantro, bound, like many of these tarts, with a flavorful custard. It's a great brunch dish. This, like most pies we bake in a tart pan, uses the very rich Pâte Brisée. It's important to have plenty of overhang when lining the pan to blind-bake the shell because the high fat content means it will shrink as it cooks. Remove the excess crust with a serrated knife after the tart is finished.

Spinach and Mushroom Galette

The galette is one of the easiest pies to make as it's simply a circle of dough—free-form, no pre-baking required. Just roll out the dough, top it like a pizza, then fold up the edges to create a rim. This peasant- or farmer-style preparation uses a simple technique to showcase the ingredients, which we think usually results in the best food. We use spinach here, but any green that sautés well, such as chard, will work.

10 ounces/285 grams Pâte Brisée (page 33)
1 ounce/30 grams unsalted butter
1 pound/450 grams button or other mushrooms, sliced
1 tablespoon minced garlic
1 tablespoon minced shallot
¼ cup/60 milliliters Madeira wine
5 ounces/140 grams spinach, stemmed and cut in a chiffonade
1 tablespoon all-purpose flour
Kosher salt and freshly ground black pepper to taste
1 ounce/30 grams Parmigiano-Reggiano cheese, grated
Egg Wash (page 28)

1. Roll out the dough to a 12-inch/30-centimeter circle on a sheet of parchment paper. Transfer the parchment and dough to a rimmed baking sheet, cover with plastic wrap, and refrigerate while you make the filling.

2. In a large skillet, melt the butter over medium-high heat. Add the mushrooms, garlic, and shallot and sauté until the mushrooms start to soften, 7 to 8 minutes. Add the Madeira and cook until the pan is almost dry, 7 to 8 minutes, then add the spinach and stir in the flour, allowing the spinach to wilt. Remove the pan from the heat. Season with salt and pepper and cool to room temperature.

3. Preheat the oven to 375°F/190°C.

4. Add the mushroom filling to the center of the dough. Spread the filling out on the dough, leaving a 2-inch/5-centimeter border. Sprinkle with the Parmigiano-Reggiano.

5. Fold the edges of the dough up over the filling to make a 10-inch/25-centimeter galette. Brush the rim of the galette with egg wash, refrigerate for 15 minutes, then egg wash again.

6. Bake until the crust is golden brown, 25 to 35 minutes. Allow it to cool slightly before cutting.

SERVES 6

This is a classic galette: cooked ingredients—here, spinach and mushrooms—are put in the center of the dough, leaving a 2-inch/5-centimeter rim, which is folded over to create the edge of the pie and hold the ingredients in (see page 123). Finished with Parmigiano-Reggiano, this pie can be served straight from the oven or at room temperature. It works well as an hors d'oeuvre or a side dish.

Stilton Cheesecake with Walnut Crust

Often in the restaurant Brian would buy a wheel or a half wheel of Stilton cheese for a buffet. More times than not, when cutting this cheese, he would end up with a pile of delicious cheese crumbs. This was expensive cheese, so he didn't want to throw them away! Thinking like a charcutier and business person, he saved all the unservable Stilton crumbs and created this decadent, savory cheesecake. And he even used a graham cracker–style crust, using walnuts and panko. That said, this is such an excellent pie, it's worth splurging on good blue cheese. This pie is excellent as an appetizer or light lunch served with a frisée salad. While you can make this in a regular tart or even pie dish, we think it's best and most elegant if you use a fluted tart pan with a removable bottom.

- 1 cup/100 grams walnut pieces
- ¾ cup/45 grams panko bread crumbs
- 6 tablespoons unsalted butter, melted
- 12 ounces/340 grams Stilton or other strong blue cheese, such as Gorgonzola or Maytag Blue
- 4 ounces/115 grams cream cheese
- ¾ cup/150 grams sour cream
- 3 tablespoons all-purpose flour
- 2 tablespoons freshly squeezed lemon juice
- 1 teaspoon vanilla extract
- 2 large eggs plus 2 large egg yolks
  Kosher salt and freshly ground black pepper to taste

1. Preheat the oven to 325°F/160°C. Spray a 10-inch/25-centimeter fluted tart pan with a removable bottom with nonstick spray.

2. To make the crust, combine the walnuts and panko in a food processor and pulse to a uniform powdery mixture.

3. Transfer the mixture to a standing mixer fitted with the paddle attachment. With the mixer running on medium, add the melted butter and mix until the panko and walnuts stick together.

4. Spread the mixture over the bottom of the prepared tart pan, packing it down for a solid base and pressing it up the sides of the pan.

5. To make the filling, combine the Stilton and cream cheese in the food processor and puree until smooth, scraping down the bowl as necessary. Add the sour cream, flour, lemon juice, and vanilla and puree until smooth. With the machine running, add the whole eggs and yolks one at a time, ensuring there are no lumps. Season with salt and pepper.

6. Pour the Stilton mixture into the crust and bake until the filling is light brown on top and set when touched, 30 to 35 minutes. Cool to room temperature before cutting.

SERVES 8

This dish goes back to Brian's days at his restaurant Pike Street. He wanted a savory cheese cake and so swapped the traditional cream cheese with Stilton. He loved the result. This pie should be thoroughly chilled so that the cuts are neat and clean. The slices should then be brought up to room temperature just as you would with any good cheese.

Summer Tomato Tart

This tart is a great way to celebrate the garden harvest of summer. Fresh, sun-soaked tomatoes have a lot of water, so slicing them, salting them, and laying them out on paper towels is an important part of the preparation. This both seasons them and concentrates their flavor. When this pie is cut, a solid wall of tomato should look impressive. Be sure to use big heirloom tomatoes, such as Brandywine or beefsteak. Once you cook onions, their color really doesn't matter from a taste standpoint—red, white, Spanish, sweet—all taste similar when cooked, so use any onion on hand. And if the season is giving you a lot of eggplant, feel free to add them to the pie (peeled, sliced, and salted, then patted dry).

- 2 tablespoons olive oil
- 1 medium onion, thinly sliced
- 4 large heirloom tomatoes, preferably a mix of red and yellow, sliced ¼ inch/6 millimeters thick
  Kosher salt and freshly ground black pepper to taste
- ¾ cup/150 grams whole-milk ricotta cheese
- 1 large egg
- ½ cup/14 grams fresh basil leaves
- 2 teaspoons freshly squeezed lemon juice
- 12 ounces/340 grams 3-2-1 Pie Dough (page 33), blind baked in a 10-inch/25-centimeter tart pan (see page 25)
- 8 ounces/225 grams buffalo mozzarella, sliced as thinly as possible
- 6 ounces/170 grams grated Parmigiano-Reggiano cheese

1. Preheat the oven to 375°F/175°C.

2. Heat the oil in a large sauté pan over medium-high heat. When the oil is hot, add the onion and sauté until it's completely cooked and tender but not browned, about 5 minutes. Transfer to a bowl and chill in the refrigerator.

3. Spread the sliced tomatoes on paper towels and season with salt and pepper.

4. Combine the ricotta, egg, basil, and lemon juice in a medium bowl, season with salt and pepper, and whisk until smooth and uniform. Stir in the cooked onion. Spread the mixture evenly in the blind-baked tart shell.

5. Shingle the sliced tomatoes on top of the ricotta mixture, then add a layer of mozzarella and Parmigiano-Reggiano. Repeat three times, finishing with a layer of tomatoes and then a sprinkle of Parmigiano-Reggiano on top to for nice browning.

6. Bake until lightly golden brown, about 25 minutes. Cool for at least 10 minutes before cutting.

SERVES 8

This is an exceptionally versatile pie as it can be served hot, at room temperature, or cold. A tart shell is blind-baked, then layered with an onion-ricotta-basil mixture, fresh mozzarella, and tomato. It can be a meal in itself or a side dish. We can't think of a more satisfying summer meal than hot buttered corn on the cob and a slice of this pie.

Sweet Potato Galette

The galette is a free-form pie that can be round, oval, square, or rectangular. It's the easiest kind of tart you can make. The idea is to roll out the dough, top it with whatever you want, then fold the edges up and over the filling by a couple inches to create a border to contain the filling. Here we're using the very rich pâte brisée dough and the nutritious sweet potato, with traditional Thanksgiving-style flavors of butter and bourbon. This is sweet and savory at the same time and would be right at home beside your roast turkey; it also makes a great side dish for pork or game. Serve hot, warm, or at room temperature.

  3 sweet potatoes (about 2½ pounds/1130 grams total)
12 ounces/340 grams Pâte Brisée (page 33)
¾ cup/165 grams light brown sugar
½ cup/120 milliliters bourbon
     Kosher salt and freshly ground black pepper to taste
  2 ounces/60 grams unsalted butter, softened and cut into bits

1. Preheat the oven to 375°F/190°C.

2. Put the sweet potatoes on a rimmed baking sheet and roast until tender; a knife inserted should meet no resistance, 45 to 60 minutes. Set aside to cool. Leave the oven on.

3. Roll out the dough to a 12-inch/30-centimeter circle on a sheet of parchment paper. Transfer the parchment and dough to a rimmed baking sheet, cover, and refrigerate while you make the filling.

4. In a small saucepan, bring the brown sugar and bourbon to a boil, then reduce to a simmer and cook until syrupy, 12 to 15 minutes. You should have ¼ to ⅓ cup/60 to 90 milliliters.

5. Peel the sweet potatoes and slice them ¼ inch/ 6 millimeters thick. Shingle the sweet potatoes around the dough, leaving a 2-inch/5-centimeter border. Season with salt and pepper. Fold the edges of the dough up over the sweet potatoes to make a 10-inch/25-centimeter galette.

6. Dot the exposed potatoes with butter and drizzle the syrup over the top.

7. Bake until the crust is golden brown, 25 to 35 minutes. Cool for at least 10 minutes before cutting.

SERVES 6

① Roll the dough out to a 12-inch/30-centimeter circle. Shingle sliced cooked sweet potatoes in a circle, leaving a 2-inch/5-centimeter border.

② Pretty much any fruit or vegetable that doesn't drop a lot of liquid when cooked (such as berries) can be turned into a galette, a simple freeform pie.

③ Dot the sweet potato with butter and bourbon syrup. Then fold the border up over the sweet potato.

④ The finished pie can be served straight from the oven or at room temperature.

The Best Mushroom Tart

This is another nonmeat pie that's perfect for brunch or as an accompaniment to a main course. Unlike the Spinach and Mushroom Galette (page 116), this one is all mushroom and is baked in a tart pan. It calls for widely available button mushrooms and shiitakes, but opt for wild mushrooms if you can. Getting a good sear on the mushrooms really adds a lot of flavor. Brian tested many different recipes for a mushroom tart in his class and came down to four different ones for the class to make and taste. This was unanimously picked as the best, thus the name!

Vegetable oil, as needed
1 pound/450 grams button mushrooms, thinly sliced
1 pound/450 grams shiitake mushrooms, stemmed and thinly sliced
2 tablespoons olive oil
¼ cup/60 grams minced shallots
Kosher salt and freshly ground black pepper to taste
½ cup/120 milliliters dry sherry
2 tablespoons all-purpose flour
1 cup/240 milliliters heavy cream
1 ounce/30 grams chopped fresh soft herbs (such as chives, flat-leaf parsley, and/or tarragon)
1 large egg, beaten
12 ounces/340 grams Pâte Brisée (page 33), blind-baked in a 10-inch/25-centimeter tart pan (see page 25)
4 ounces/115 grams grated Parmigiano-Reggiano cheese

1. Set a heavy-bottomed sauté pan over high heat and allow it to get hot. Add enough vegetable oil to coat the bottom (if your pan is hot enough, the oil will swirl and just smoke). Add one-third of the mushrooms and press down hard on them with a spatula to brown them, 7 to 8 minutes. Transfer to a large bowl and repeat with the remaining two batches.

2. In the same pan (wipe it out if necessary), heat the olive oil over medium heat. Return all of the mushrooms to the pan, along with the shallots, and season with salt and pepper. Add the sherry and reduce it until it's almost all evaporated, 6 to 8 minutes.

3. Sprinkle the flour over the mushrooms and stir to incorporate it. Add the cream and reduce by about half, 7 to 8 minutes. Stir in the herbs, then remove the pan from the heat and allow it to cool to room temperature.

4. Preheat the oven to 350°F/175°C.

5. Stir the egg into the mushrooms. Transfer the mixture to the blind-baked tart shell. Top with the Parmigiano-Reggiano.

6. Bake until it's set, about 20 minutes. Cool before cutting.

SERVES 6

The excess dough has been cut from the cooled **mushroom tart**, and the tart has been removed from the fluted tart pan and sliced while cold for cleaner cuts. It can be eaten at room temperature but is best reheated in a 350°F/175°C oven for 10 to 15 minutes.

DOUBLE-CRUSTED PIES

Tomato, Basil, and Mozzarella Pie   130

Post-Thanksgiving Turkey Pot Pie   133

American Pekin Duck Pie with Pistachios   134

Braised Pork and Lentil Pie   138

Pork and Duck Confit Pie   139

Chicken Sheet Pan Pie   140

Chicken, Mushroom, and Bacon Sheet Pan Pie   143

Atlantic Salmon in Puff Pastry   144

Individual Duck Confit Pies   146

Individual Pot Roast Pies with Roasted Carrots and Caramelized Onions   149

A traditional turkey pot pie (page 133).

There are various types of double-crusted pies, which is why this is one of the biggest chapters in the book. They can be cooked in a pie plate, on a sheet pan, or simply individually shaped, with a flat crust on the bottom, topped with filling, and covered with a second layer of dough. You can even use a fluted tart pan.

As noted earlier, it's believed that the sweet fruit pie came to dominate pies in America in the mid-nineteenth century when the sugar business boomed, which allowed us to take advantage of the abundant stone fruits, apples, and berries that grow here. But the double-crusted pie is just as excellent for savory pies.

These can be liquidy inside, like the Post-Thanksgiving Turkey Pot Pie, or firm and sliceable, like the Pork and Duck Confit Pie. The latter you can think of almost as an informal pâté en croûte, with a forcemeat and delicious inlays.

We especially love sheet pan pies, made on a quarter sheet pan. These are simple, easily shaped, and delicious, and make a great presentation.

3-2-1 Pie Dough (page 33), prepared for **American Pekin Duck Pie** (page 134).

Tomato, Basil, and Mozzarella Pie

This pie is all about the tomato and differs from the Summer Tomato Tart (page 120) in a few ways, the most notable difference being the crust. Tomatoes in a crust are surprisingly delicious—perhaps because the juiciness of the tomatoes enhances the crust. This pie uses puff pastry rather than a standard pie dough, and it is partially covered using a lattice crust. If you have a lattice cutter (see page 20), by all means use that. If you don't, cut the second half of the dough into ½-inch/1.25-centimeter strips. A lattice top allows the tomatoes' moisture to evaporate while the crust stays crisp. If you have access to water buffalo mozzarella, that's the best; otherwise any fresh mozzarella will work.

1¼ pounds/570 grams Blitz Puff Pastry Dough (page 36) or 4 sheets store-bought puff pastry, thawed in the refrigerator
3 tablespoons olive oil
1 pound/450 grams sweet onions, julienned
2 pounds/900 grams heirloom tomatoes (about 4 large tomatoes), cut into wedges and seeded
   Kosher salt and freshly ground black pepper to taste
8 ounces/225 grams fresh mozzarella, sliced ¼ inch/6 millimeters thick
1 cup/20 grams fresh basil leaves, roughly chopped
   Egg Wash (page 28)

1. Divide the dough in half and roll out each piece on a sheet of parchment paper to a rectangle 8 by 14 inches/20 by 35 centimeters. Stack the parchment and dough on a rimmed baking sheet, cover with plastic wrap, and refrigerate.

2. In a large sauté pan, heat 2 tablespoons olive oil over medium heat. When the oil is hot, add the onions and sauté until soft but not browned, 12 to 15 minutes. Set aside to cool.

3. Put the tomatoes in a large bowl and season with salt and pepper. Toss them to distribute the seasoning, then spread them out on paper towels to drain.

4. Put the mozzarella in a medium bowl. Season with salt and pepper. Add the basil and remaining 1 tablespoon olive oil and toss to distribute.

5. Preheat the oven to 375°F/190°C.

6. On one dough rectangle, arrange the tomatoes in a single layer, leaving a 1-inch/2.5-centimeter border. Lay the cheese slices on the tomatoes, then spread the sautéed onions over the top, pressing down lightly on them. Egg wash the dough border.

7. Cut the second dough rectangle with a lattice cutter. Allow the dough to soften to the point that you can spread the pattern out, then place it on top of the pie. (Or cut the dough into ½-inch/1.25-centimeter strips, using a fluted pastry wheel if you have one. Lay the strips diagonally over the pie for a proper lattice top.) Press the two doughs together along the edge, then trim any overhanging dough. Roll the edge over to crimp and seal it. Egg wash the entire pie, chill it for 20 minutes, then egg wash it a second time.

8. Bake until the top is golden brown, 35 to 45 minutes. Let cool for at least 15 minutes before cutting.

SERVES 8

The great feature of this double-crusted pie—tomato, onion, basil, and mozzarella—is the lattice crust, which is both decorative and allows for plenty of evaporation during baking. A good lattice crust, made with a lattice cutter, is all about temperature. You must cut the dough when it is thoroughly chilled so that the cuts are distinct. The dough should then temper for 10 minutes or so at room temperature so the dough is pliable. If the dough is too warm when you cut it, the cuts can stick together. If you try to spread the lattice out when it's too cold, it can break. Also, depending on the sharpness of your lattice cutter, you may need to go over the cuts with a paring knife.

Post-Thanksgiving Turkey Pot Pie

We've put this recipe here because, unlike the pot pies in the first chapter, this is a traditional pot pie with a bottom crust and a top crust, making it a double-crusted pie. This pot pie uses the carcass of the holiday bird to make a rich turkey stock. Making stock is a very flexible process, so use common sense rather than precise measurements. Of course it's fine to use store-bought turkey stock, but homemade is so much better and takes less than 10 minutes of active time. It's well worth the small effort, since the turkey is abundance itself and shouldn't be wasted.

- 2 ounces/60 grams unsalted butter
- 1 medium onion, cut into medium dice
- 4 garlic cloves, roughly chopped
  Kosher salt to taste
- 2 carrots, cut into medium dice
- 2 celery ribs, cut crosswise into ¼-inch/ 6-millimeter pieces
- 6 tablespoons/45 grams all-purpose flour
- 2½ cups/600 milliliters Turkey Stock (recipe follows)
- 2½ cups/450 grams shredded or diced cooked turkey
- ½ cup/75 grams fresh or frozen peas
- ¼ cup/60 milliliters heavy cream
- 1 tablespoon fish sauce
- ½ teaspoon freshly ground black pepper
- 1½ pounds/680 grams 3-2-1 Pie Dough (page 33) or 2 sheets store-bought pie dough, thawed if frozen
- 1 large egg mixed with 1 tablespoon milk

1. Preheat the oven to 350°F/175°C.

2. Melt the butter in a large saucepan over medium-high heat. Add the onion and garlic, hit them with a four-finger pinch of salt, and cook until tender, 3 to 4 minutes. Add the carrots and celery and cook until they are heated and brightly colored, 3 to 4 minutes. Add the flour and stir to cook the flour and ensure it's well coated with butter. Add the stock, whisking to ensure the flour doesn't clump. Bring the mixture to a simmer, then add the turkey, peas, cream, fish sauce, and pepper and mix well. Remove the pan from the heat. Cool to room temperature or chill in the refrigerator after.

3. Divide the dough in half. Roll out one half to line a 9-inch/23-centimeter pie plate (or use one sheet of store-bought dough).

4. Roll out the other piece of dough to your desired thinness for the top of the pie. Fill the pie shell with the turkey mixture. Cover it with the top piece of dough and pinch the edges around the rim to seal it. Brush the top with egg wash, then cut several steam holes.

5. Bake until the filling is piping hot and the crust has browned, about 45 minutes. Let it rest for 5 to 10 minutes before serving.

SERVES 6

Turkey Stock

- Leftover roast turkey bones
- 1 onion, quartered
- 2 or 3 carrots, cut into 2 or 3 pieces
- 2 to 3 tablespoons tomato paste (optional)
  Flat-leaf parsley sprigs (optional)
  Thyme sprigs (optional)
  Whole black peppercorns (optional)

1. Preheat the oven to 200°F/95°C.

2. Combine all the ingredients in a large stockpot, then fill the pot with water. Put the pot in the oven, uncovered, for 8 hours. (Alternatively, fill a large stockpot with the turkey bones, cover with water, and simmer very gently on the stovetop, uncovered, for 3 hours. Discard the bones, then add the remaining ingredients and simmer, uncovered, for 45 minutes.)

3. Strain into a large bowl or pot.

American Pekin Duck Pie
with Pistachios

Pekin ducks came to America from China in the mid-1800s and continue to account for half the domestic ducks eaten in the US. The famous Long Island duck comes from this breed. All the meat is dark and mild in taste, and the fat is delicious. Just about any meat market will carry Pekin ducks, but they may be frozen, so thaw them slowly in the refrigerator over a couple of days. D'Artagnan is a good online source for a range of ducks and duck products, plus many other meats and sausages. (Wild ducks such as mallards can be used in this pie, but the meat is much stronger in flavor and will require more condiments such as chutney and pickles to offset the gamy taste.)

While this recipe isn't difficult, there are a lot of steps, starting with breaking down and boning out a duck. If you don't feel comfortable breaking down the duck, or simply need to reduce the time you spend, ask your butcher to do it for you as described below. (Be sure to reserve the skin and fat for rendering and the bones for stock!)

Duck makes for an extraordinary pie, cooked in a tart shell that's topped with a layer of the dough—a kind of rough pâté en croûte. Serve hot with Red Currant Sauce (page 193) or cold with some good mustard, such as either of the Hot Mustards (page 191).

 1 (5-pound/2.25-kilogram) Pekin duck
10 ounces/285 grams pork back fat, diced
    Kosher salt and freshly ground black pepper
    to taste
 2 tablespoons vegetable oil
 2 tablespoons minced garlic
 2 tablespoons minced shallot
¼ cup/60 milliliters Madeira wine
 2 large eggs
½ cup/65 grams shelled pistachios, coarsely
    chopped
 1 cup/140 grams small-diced smoked ham
1¾ pounds/795 grams 3-2-1 Pie Dough (page 33)
    Egg Wash (page 28)

BREAK DOWN THE DUCK

1. Remove the wings and set aside for stock.

2. Remove the neck, gizzard, and liver from the cavity. Add the neck and gizzard to the wings for stock, and set aside the liver.

3. Remove the legs and thighs from the carcass, then remove each breast. Put the carcass with the wings, neck, and gizzard.

4. Remove all excess skin and fat from the leg, thigh, and breast pieces. Combine all the fat and skin in a pile. Remove the meat from the leg and thigh bones.

5. Weigh the leg and thigh meat; there should be about 12 ounces/340 grams. (If you don't have quite enough, add diced pork shoulder to make up the difference.) Set the meat aside.

6. Remove and discard all sinew from the breasts. Save for stock.

7. Remove and discard the heavy veins in the liver and put the liver with the breasts.

> *Note:* When you (or your butcher) have finished butchering the duck, you should have four piles (or bags):
>
> 1. Wings, neck, gizzard, and carcass (to make stock)
> 2. Leg and thigh meat
> 3. Fat and skin (to render for another use, if desired—combine with 3 tablespoons water in a small baking pan and heat in a 325°F/160°C oven for 20 to 30 minutes)
> 4. Breasts and liver

MAKE THE PIE

1. Combine the duck leg and thigh meat with the pork fat and grind through an ⅛-inch/3-millimeter die into a large bowl. Season with salt and pepper. Cover and refrigerate.

2. Season the duck breasts and liver with salt and pepper.

3. Heat the oil in a large sauté pan over high heat until it's almost smoking. Sear the breasts and liver, leaving the centers raw, 3 to 4 minutes per side. Transfer the breasts and liver to a plate, cover, and refrigerate.

4. Turn the heat down to medium, add the garlic and shallot to the pan, and cook until softened, making sure not to brown them, about 5 minutes. Deglaze the pan with the Madeira and reduce until almost dry, 7 to 8 minutes. Scrape the contents of the pan onto a plate to cool.

5. In a food processor, combine the chilled ground meat, eggs, and cooled garlic-shallot reduction and puree until smooth. Do not over-puree; if the meat goes above 45°F/7°C, the fat can break out of it and the texture will be off. Transfer the puree to a large bowl and fold in the pistachios and ham. Cook a tablespoon of the mixture in a small pan, taste, and adjust the seasoning as necessary. Cover and refrigerate.

6. Preheat the oven to 400°F/205°C.

7. Weigh out 1 pound/450 grams of the dough and roll into a 12-inch/30-centimeter circle. Use the dough to line the bottom of a 10-inch/25-centimeter tart pan with a removable bottom. Make sure to tuck the dough all the way into the corners and leave about a 1-inch/2.5-centimeter overhang.

8. Spread one-third of the pureed meat mixture in the tart shell. Cut the duck breasts in half lengthwise, then press them into the meat mixture in a circle pattern. Spread another third of the meat mixture over the breasts. Cut the liver into bite-size pieces, then press them into the meat mixture, spacing them evenly. Cover with the remaining meat mixture, making sure the livers are covered completely.

9. Roll the remaining dough into an 11-inch/28-centimeter circle for the lid (reserving a scrap to use to make the chimney ring). Moisten the bottom crust overhang with water, then place the lid on top, pinching the bottom and top layers of dough together to seal. Fold the dough under itself all the way around the edge. Using the three-finger method (see page 30), crimp the edge all the way around.

10. Cut a vent hole in the center of the pie, 1½ inches/3.75 centimeters in diameter. Roll out the reserved scrap of dough and cut a ring 2 inches/5 centimeters in diameter. Then cut a 1½-inch/3.75-centimeter hole in the center of the 2-inch/5-centimeter dough disc to make a doughnut shape that will fit around the vent hole and support the chimney. Fashion an aluminum foil chimney, 1½ inches/3.75 centimeters in diameter, and fit it into the vent hole.

11. Egg wash the top of the pie, being careful not to let it pool, refrigerate for 15 minutes, and egg wash again. If you have leftover dough, you can roll it out and cut leaves for decoration or score the top with a sharp knife.

12. Bake the pie until the crust browns, 15 to 20 minutes. Turn the oven temperature down to 325°F/160°C and bake to an internal temperature of 135°F/57°C. Allow to rest for 15 to 20 minutes before cutting.

SERVES 6

① To begin the duck pie, line the tart pan with dough and have its top ready. Put in a layer of the duck and pork forcemeat and spread it evenly across the bottom.

② Add a layer of seared breast and seared liver to cover the forcemeat.

③ Spread a second layer of forcemeat over the breast and liver.

④ Moisten the edges of the lid with water. Place on top of pie. Pinch the two doughs together. Roll the edge over itself forming a bead. Crimp using the three-finger method (page 30).

Here is a double-crusted meat pie—a duck and pork forcemeat inlaid with seared duck breast and seared duck liver. It's best served hot with Red Currant Sauce (page 193) but can also be served at room temperature with some good mustard.

Braised Pork and Lentil Pie

This pie came about in order to make use of leftovers. Brian had some pork stew he'd made for the family, as well as some cooked lentils. Pork and beans are always a great combination! It was so good he decided to make it into its own pie. Make sure the sauce is thick enough to bind the ingredients, like a heavy gravy, so it doesn't weep when the pie is cut. This recipe calls for green lentils, but any kind will work, though they may require a different cook time.

1½ pounds/680 grams lean pork shoulder, cut into ½-inch/1.25-centimeter dice
   Kosher salt and freshly ground black pepper to taste
3 tablespoons vegetable oil
¾ cup/112 grams small-diced onion
1 tablespoon minced garlic
1 tablespoon tomato paste
½ cup/120 milliliters dry red wine
1¼ cups/300 milliliters rich veal stock or high-quality beef stock
¼ cup/50 grams green lentils
½ cup/112 grams small-diced carrots
¼ cup beurre manié (see page 46), or as needed
   Egg Wash (page 28)
1 pound 6 ounces/625 grams 3-2-1 Pie Dough (page 33)

1. Season the pork all over with salt and pepper. Heat the oil in a large, heavy-bottomed sauté pan over medium-high heat. When the oil is hot, brown the meat on all sides in small batches. Transfer the meat to a plate lined with paper towels.

2. In the same pan, sauté the onion and garlic over medium heat until soft, about 3 minutes. Add the tomato paste and cook until browned, 2 to 3 minutes. Deglaze the pan with the wine and reduce until the pan is almost dry, 6 to 8 minutes. Add 1 cup/240 milliliters stock and bring it to a simmer. Return the pork to the pan, turn the heat down to low, cover, and gently simmer (do not boil) until the meat is tender, about 1 hour.

3. Meanwhile, put the lentils in a small saucepan, cover with water, season with salt, and simmer until almost tender, about 20 minutes. Add the carrots and cook until both are soft, about 10 minutes. Drain and set aside.

4. When the pork is tender, strain the cooking liquid into a large saucepan and bring to a simmer. Add the beurre manié and whisk until it's incorporated. The sauce should be smooth and thick enough to coat the meat evenly. Season with salt and pepper. Add the meat, lentils, and carrots, cover, and chill completely.

5. Preheat the oven to 375°F/190°C.

6. Divide the dough roughly into a 12-ounce/340-gram piece for the bottom and a 10-ounce/285-gram piece for the top. Roll the bottom dough into a circle just larger than a 9-inch-23-centimeter pie plate. Line the pie plate with the dough. There should be about a ½-inch/1.25-centimeter overhang. Fill the shell evenly with the meat filling.

7. Roll the second piece of dough into a 9-inch/23-centimeter circle for the lid. Moisten the bottom crust overhang with water, pinching the bottom and top layers of dough together to seal. Fold the dough under itself all the way around the edge. Using the three-finger method (see page 30), crimp the edge all the way around. Egg wash, refrigerate for 15 minutes, then egg wash again. With a pair of scissors, snip vent holes in the top.

8. Bake until the top is golden brown and the filling is bubbling, 35 to 45 minutes. Allow to cool for 15 minutes before cutting.

SERVES 4 TO 6

Pork and Duck Confit Pie

This is an especially meaty pie, a simplified version of a pâté en croûte, with chunks of duck confit serving as an interior garnish within the ground pork. Grated potato helps hold it all together, with moisture from onion and mushrooms. Serve slices of this pie hot or cold, with horseradish and Colman's mustard on the side.

- 3 duck legs confit
- 1 ounce/30 grams unsalted butter or confit fat
- 1 cup/135 grams small-diced onion
- 3 tablespoons minced garlic
- 1½ cups/240 grams quartered button mushrooms
- 1 cup/110 grams grated russet potato, squeezed dry
- ½ cup/120 milliliters dry white wine
  Kosher salt and freshly ground black pepper to taste
- 1 pound/450 grams ground pork
- ¼ cup/14 grams chopped fresh flat-leaf parsley
- 1 pound/450 grams 3-2-1 Pie Dough (page 33)
  Egg Wash (page 28)

1. Preheat the oven to 350°F/175°C.

2. Put the confit in a cast-iron or other oven-safe skillet and warm in the oven for 15 minutes so that the excess fat melts. Remove and turn the oven temperature up to 400°F/205°C.

3. Meanwhile, melt the butter in a large, heavy-bottomed sauté pan over medium heat. Add the onion and garlic and cook until soft, 3 to 4 minutes. Add the mushrooms and potato and cook until dry, about 5 minutes. Add the wine to deglaze the pan. Season with salt and pepper and set aside to cool completely.

4. Pick all the duck meat from the skin and bones (reserve the skin and bones for another use). Cut the meat into 1-inch/2.5-centimeter dice.

5. Combine the duck, ground pork, and parsley in a large bowl and season with salt and pepper. Add the cooled onion mixture and mix until all the ingredients are evenly distributed.

6. Divide the dough in half. Roll out one piece into an 11-inch/28-centimeter circle. Line a 9-inch/23-centimeter pie plate with the dough. Trim the dough so you have a uniform 1-inch/2.5-centimeter overhang.

7. Roll out the second piece of dough into a 10-inch/25-centimeter circle and set it aside.

8. Fill the pie shell with the meat mixture, patting it down to avoid air pockets. Moisten the edge of the dough with water. Top the pie with the second piece of dough. Crimp the edges using the three-finger method (see page 30). Egg wash the top, refrigerate for 15 minutes, then egg wash again. Cut slits in the top for ventilation.

9. Bake for 30 minutes. Turn the oven temperature down to 350°F/175°C and continue baking until the top is golden brown and the filling is bubbly, 20 to 30 minutes more.

SERVES 6

Chicken Sheet Pan Pie

This sheet pan pie (pictured on page 8) makes a dramatic presentation, especially if you take the time to decorate the top with dough scraps. And it's especially suited to larger gatherings. It's best to serve this pie on a big cutting board, both for presentation and for ease of cutting. We like to pair this dish with a creamy mushroom sauce or even Mushroom Jus Lié (page 196), or rich Chicken Stock (page 189) thickened with beurre manié. The filling is essentially chicken sausage, but we've amped up the flavor with bacon, roasted garlic, and fresh herbs, and onion helps keep it moist without adding more fat. If you don't have a meat grinder or want to save time, simply ask your butcher to grind the chicken thighs with the bacon.

14	ounces/400 grams boneless skinless chicken thighs, cut in large dice
	Kosher salt and freshly ground black pepper to taste
6	ounces/170 grams slab bacon, cut in large dice
2	tablespoons vegetable oil
8	ounces/225 grams boneless, skinless chicken breasts, cut in large dice
1	cup/220 grams diced sweet onion
¼	cup/60 milliliters dry white wine
¼	cup/14 grams fresh flat-leaf parsley, coarsely chopped
2	tablespoons roasted garlic (see page 71)
1	tablespoon fresh thyme leaves
1½	pounds/680 grams 3-2-1 Pie Dough (page 33)
	Egg Wash (page 28)

1. In a medium bowl, season the chicken thighs all over with salt, add the bacon, and season it all with pepper. Cover and refrigerate until ready to grind.

2. Heat the oil in a large, heavy-bottomed sauté pan over medium-high heat. When the oil is hot, brown the diced chicken breast on all sides, leaving the center raw, 1 to 2 minutes. Transfer to a plate lined with paper towels. Turn the heat down to medium, add the onion, and sauté until soft but with very little color. Deglaze the pan with the wine and reduce to a syrup, 6 to 8 minutes. Scrape the contents of the pan onto a plate, cover, and refrigerate until thoroughly chilled.

3. Preheat the oven to 375°F/190°C.

4. Add the chilled onion, parsley, roasted garlic, and thyme to the bowl with the chicken thigh and bacon. Grind it through a ⅜-inch/9-millimeter die into a large bowl. Mix by hand or with a wooden spoon until well blended. Cook a tablespoon of the mixture in a small pan, taste, and adjust the seasoning as necessary. Fold in the browned chicken breast.

5. Divide the dough in half. Roll out each piece into a 9 by 12-inch/23 by 3-centimeter rectangle (reserving a scrap to use to make the chimney ring). Line a rimmed baking sheet with parchment paper and place one piece of dough on it. Spread the ground meat mixture over the dough, leaving a 1½-inch/3.75-centimeter border of dough uncovered. Moisten the border of the bottom dough with water, then top it with the second piece of dough. Press the dough to seal it, then use the three-finger method (see page 30) to crimp the edges all around.

6. Cut a vent hole in the center of the pie, 1½ inches/3.75 centimeters in diameter. Fashion an aluminum foil chimney, 1½ inches/3.75 centimeters in diameter, and fit it into the vent hole (pictured on page 27). Roll out the reserved scrap of dough and cut a ring the diameter of your chimney to go around the chimney for support. Brush it with egg wash and place around the vent hole.

7. Egg wash the top of the pie, being careful not to let it pool, refrigerate for 15 minutes, and egg wash again.

8. Bake the pie to an internal temperature of 160°F/71°C, 30 to 45 minutes. Allow it to rest for 15 minutes before cutting.

SERVES 6

Mashed potatoes and gravy are the quintessential pairing for pies, especially for this chicken, mushroom, and bacon double-crusted pie.

Chicken, Mushroom, and Bacon Sheet Pan Pie

When it comes to cooking, you really can't *teach* someone to do it. You can demonstrate method and technique, but it's up to the individual to process the information and use their taste imagination to move forward. With that in mind, you develop recipes based on your experience and acquired skill.

At Schoolcraft College, Brian and his colleagues often do research and development. Brian's officemate Drew, who recently passed the arduous Certified Master Chef exam, had a consulting job with a successful barbecue restaurant in Detroit that has multiple outlets. One of their popular sandwiches contained chicken, bacon, mushroom, mustard, and cheese. They asked Drew to develop a sausage with the same flavor profile as a new menu item. Again, Schoolcraft is a rare environment of talented professionals who share and grow as cooks and chefs. Brian offered Drew his class for the research and development (as sausage making is one of the key techniques he teaches). After five or six iterations, they came up with a great sausage. It was so good, Brian thought, why not put it in a pie?

    1 ounce/30 grams unsalted butter
    8 ounces/225 grams button mushrooms, cut into
      large pieces
 1½ pounds/680 grams boneless, skinless chicken
      thighs, cut into large dice
    8 ounces/225 grams slab bacon, cut into large
      dice
    8 ounces/225 grams fatty pork shoulder or belly,
      cut into large dice
 1½ tablespoons kosher salt
    1 tablespoon toasted brown mustard seeds
 2½ teaspoons ground white pepper
    2 teaspoons Colman's mustard powder
 ½ teaspoon ground mace
 ½ teaspoon ground ginger
 1½ pounds/680 grams Pâte Brisée (page 33)
      Egg Wash (page 28)

1. Preheat the oven to 375°F/190°C.

2. Melt the butter in a large sauté pan over medium-high heat. Add the mushrooms and cook until soft, 10 to 12 minutes. Transfer to a plate to cool.

3. Combine the chicken, bacon, pork, salt, mustard seeds, white pepper, dry mustard, mace, and ginger and grind through a 3/16-inch/5-millimeter die into a large bowl.

4. With your hands, vigorously mix the meat and seasoning to create a primary bind. Take a ball of meat, smaller than a golf ball, and squeeze it in your hand to make a tight ball. Lay your hand out flat and turn it upside down—the meat should stick to your hand for at least 10 seconds (if it doesn't, give it another mix until it does). Cook a tablespoon of the mixture in a small pan, taste, and adjust the seasoning as necessary.

5. Divide the dough in half. Roll out each piece to a 9 by 12-inch/23 by 30-centimeter rectangle. Line a rimmed baking sheet with parchment paper and place one piece of dough on it. Spread the ground meat mixture over the dough, leaving a 1½-inch/3.75-centimeter border of dough uncovered. Moisten the border of the bottom dough with water, then top it with the second piece of dough and press the edges of the dough together. With a pastry wheel or knife, cut the corners off at a 45-degree angle (to eliminate unnecessary dough). Press the dough to seal it, then use the three-finger method (see page 30) to crimp the edges all around.

6. Egg wash the top, refrigerate for 15 minutes, and egg wash again. Cut two vent holes in the top.

7. Bake until the internal temperature reaches 160°F/71°C, 30 to 45 minutes. Allow it to rest for 15 minutes before cutting.

SERVES 8

Atlantic Salmon in Puff Pastry

Among the most famous salmon dishes in the classical French repertoire is coulibiac, from the Russian kulebyáka, a hot fish pie layered with rice, hard-cooked egg, mushrooms, dill, cabbage, onion, and vesiga (the marrow of the sturgeon spine). Escoffier brought the dish to France in the early 1900s, Frenchifying the name and including a version in *Le Guide Culinaire* that used halibut wrapped in brioche dough (in Russia it would have been salmon or sturgeon). This version hews more closely to the original Russian, using cooked rice and hard-cooked eggs.

Traditionally, coulibiac is sliced and served with melted butter—and there's no reason you couldn't go this route—but a lightly thickened fish fumet using cornstarch or arrowroot, finished with a touch of cream, also works well. This is a labor-intensive dish that makes a dramatic centerpiece to a meal for any occasion.

6 ounces/170 grams spinach leaves

1 ounce/30 grams unsalted butter

6 ounces/170 grams button mushrooms, thinly sliced

2 tablespoons minced shallot

¼ cup/60 milliliters dry sherry

½ cup/120 milliliters heavy cream
Kosher salt and freshly ground black pepper to taste

½ cup/85 grams cooked white rice

3 tablespoons fresh dill leaves

10 ounces/300 grams Blitz Puff Pastry Dough (page 36) or 2 sheets store-bought puff pastry, thawed in the refrigerator

4 (10-inch/25-centimeter) Crêpes (page 27)

3 large hard-cooked eggs, sliced ⅛ inch/3 milliliters thick (use an egg slicer if you have one)

1½ pounds/680 grams center-cut Atlantic salmon, about 14 by 4 inches/35 by 10 centimeters
Egg Wash (page 28)

1. Pour about ¼ inch/6 millimeters water into a medium pot. Heat the water over high heat, then add the spinach and toss with tongs. Cover and cook for 1 minute, then uncover and toss the spinach so that it all starts to wilt. Cover again and finish wilting, another minute or so. Remove from the heat, uncover, and let rest until it's cool enough to handle. Wring out the spinach and set it aside.

2. Melt the butter in a large sauté pan over medium-high heat. Add the mushrooms and shallot and cook until almost all the mushroom liquid has cooked off, 8 to 10 minutes. Add the sherry and reduce until dry, 7 to 8 minutes. Add the cream, bring to a simmer, season with salt and pepper, and cook until the sauce coats the back of a spoon, 7 to 8 minutes. Transfer to a medium bowl and cool to room temperature. Once cool, add the rice and dill and mix well.

3. Preheat the oven to 400°F/205°C. Line a rimmed baking sheet with parchment paper.

4. Roll out the pastry into a 16 by 8-inch/40 by 20-centimeter rectangle. Lay two crêpes side by side on the dough, slightly overlapping. Lay the spinach lengthwise down the middle of the crêpes, creating a 14 by 4-inch/35 by 10-centimeter strip. Shingle the sliced eggs on top of the spinach. Spread the mushroom-rice mixture over the eggs in an even layer.

5. Pat the salmon dry with paper towels, season with salt and pepper, and place on top of the rice; nestle it down so there are no air pockets.

6. Fold half of the dough over the fish, moisten the edge with egg wash, and fold the other half over, creating a seal down the middle. Carefully flip the pie over onto the lined baking sheet so the seam is on the bottom. Trim the ends and fold them under. Brush the top with egg wash, refrigerate for 15 to 20 minutes, then egg wash again.

7. Bake until golden brown, about 20 minutes, then turn the oven temperature down to 350°F/175°C and continue baking until the internal temperature reaches 120°F/48°C, another 15 to 25 minutes. Allow to rest for 15 minutes before cutting.

SERVES 6

Individual Duck Confit Pies

These are great as an appetizer or an accompaniment to a salad course and can be put together fast for a tasty, crusty, substantial bite in a hurry. The flaky crust and rich confit together are delicious—we'd be surprised if the dish didn't spark a conversation about the simplicity of ingredients relative to their sheer deliciousness. There's a duck confit recipe in *Charcuterie*, and Michael has posted on his site about making duck confit with olive oil, but you can also buy duck confit online from D'Artagnan. We always prefer homemade pastry for flavor, but store-bought pie dough can be used if you roll it thinly as instructed below.

    3 duck legs confit
    ¼ cup/20 grams thinly sliced scallions
       Kosher salt and freshly ground pepper to taste
    10 ounces/280 grams Pâte Brisée (page 33)
       Egg Wash (page 28)

1. Preheat the oven to 350°F/175°C.

2. Put the confit in a cast-iron or other oven-safe skillet and warm in the oven for 15 minutes so that the excess fat melts. Remove and turn the oven temperature up to 400°F/205°C.

3. Pick all the meat from the bones and the skin. Chop the meat finely. If you wish, chop the skin to a paste and toss this with the meat. Add just enough fat from the skillet to moisten the meat. Stir in the scallions. Taste and add salt and pepper if needed.

4. Roll out the dough into an ⅛-inch/3-millimeter thick circle. Using a biscuit cutter, cut out six 4-inch/10-centimeter circles and six 3½-inch/9-centimeter circles. Place the six larger circles on a rimmed baking sheet.

5. Divide the filling evenly between the six larger circles and egg wash the edges. Place a smaller circle on top of each. Fold the larger edge over the smaller and crimp using the three-finger method (see page 30), yielding six pleats. Egg wash the top and pleats, refrigerate for 20 minutes, and egg wash a second time.

6. Bake until crisp and brown, 15 to 20 minutes. Let rest for 5 minutes before serving.

SERVES 6

These are mini two-crusted pies. Put a little shredded duck confit meat in the middle of a small circle of Pâte Brisée, egg wash the rim, put a circle on top, press to seal, then pinch six points into a star shape. These make a fun side dish, or terrific hors d'oeuvres. They travel well and are quickly reheated in a friend's oven. Served here with Apricot and Sweet Onion Chutney (page 196).

"I created this pie," Brian says, "and I'm particularly proud of it. It's a classic American dish, pot roast with mashed potatoes and vegetables, reimagined as a pie. Everything is cooked ahead so this finishes quickly in the oven, allowing you to achieve that gorgeous golden-brown crust.

"When I'm teaching my students this pie, I tell them to *butter* the carrots with the mashed potatoes, that's how they should be applied, to ensure the potato fills in all the spaces between the carrots. The potatoes are topped with spinach and caramelized onions."

Individual Pot Roast Pies
with Roasted Carrots and Caramelized Onions

These individual double-crusted pies have all the flavor and rib-sticking deliciousness of a classic American pot roast. The construction of the pie is visually dramatic, with the pot roast on the bottom, topped with carrots, potatoes, onion, and spinach. It's bound with thickened braising liquid and served with more of the gravy-like braising liquid.

The preparation is lengthy but worth it, as all the components are cooked separately, cooled, and then assembled. It's best to start this recipe a day ahead, and in fact the meat can be cooked and refrigerated up to 5 days in advance. On the other hand, these pies are the perfect vehicle for leftover pot roast and mashed potatoes, in which case the preparation goes very quickly.

FOR THE POT ROAST

- 1 pound/450 grams lean pot roast from the shoulder clod or plate (often labeled chuck roast)
  Kosher salt and freshly ground black pepper to taste
  All-purpose flour, for dredging
  Vegetable oil, for sautéing
- ¾ cup/90 grams small diced onion
- ½ cup/60 grams small diced carrot
- ½ cup/60 grams small diced celery
- 2 garlic cloves, peeled
- 1 tablespoon tomato paste
- ½ cup/120 milliliters dry red wine
- 2 cups/475 milliliters veal or beef stock
- 4 thyme sprigs
- 8 whole black peppercorns
- 1 bay leaf
- 2 tablespoons cornstarch slurry or beurre manié (see page 46), or as needed

FOR THE CARROTS

- 4 carrots (about 6 inches/15 centimeters long and about 1 inch/2.5 centimeters in diameter at the large end), peeled
- 2 tablespoons olive oil
  Kosher salt and freshly ground black pepper to taste

FOR THE CARAMELIZED ONIONS

- 2 ounces/60 grams unsalted butter
- 1 pound/450 grams onions, thinly sliced
  Kosher salt and freshly ground black pepper to taste

FOR THE POTATOES

- 8 ounces/235 grams russet potatoes
- 1 ounce/28 grams unsalted butter, at room temperature
- ¼ cup/60 milliliters heavy cream or whole milk, warmed
  Kosher salt and freshly ground black pepper to taste

FOR THE WILTED SPINACH

- 2 ounces/60 grams spinach leaves, stems removed

TO FINISH THE PIE

- 10 ounces/280 grams 3-2-1 Pie Dough (page 33)
  Egg Wash (page 28)

(recipe continues)

MAKE THE POT ROAST

1. Preheat the oven to 325°F/160°C.

2. Season the meat all over with salt and pepper, then dredge in flour. Pour about ¼ inch/8 millimeters vegetable oil into a large Dutch oven and heat over medium-high heat. When the oil is hot, brown the meat on all sides, 2 to 3 minutes per side. Transfer the meat to a plate lined with paper towels.

3. Pour off the excess oil from the Dutch oven, leaving a thin coat. (If the flour has burned, wipe out the pot and add a thin coat of fresh vegetable oil.) Heat the oil over medium heat. When the oil is hot, add the onion, carrot, celery, and garlic cloves and cook until tender, 6 to 8 minutes. Turn the heat up to medium-high and brown the vegetables, 4 to 5 minutes. Clear a spot in the middle, add the tomato paste, and let it cook and brown for 1 to 2 minutes.

4. Deglaze the pan with half of the red wine, then allow it to reduce to a syrup, 4 to 5 minutes. Add the remaining wine and allow this to reduce to syrup, about 5 minutes. Add the stock, thyme, peppercorns, and bay and bring it to a simmer.

5. Return the meat to the pot, cover the pot, and put it in the oven for 2 to 3 hours, until the meat is tender.

6. Using a slotted spoon, transfer the meat to a bowl and set aside to cool. (If making ahead, refrigerate in an airtight container.)

7. Strain the liquid in the pot into a medium saucepan (discard the solids) and reduce over high heat until thick, 6 to 8 minutes. It should easily coat the back of a spoon. If it remains too thin, thicken it with a cornstarch slurry or beurre manié. Set aside to cool. (If making ahead, refrigerate in a separate airtight container.)

MAKE THE CARROTS

1. Preheat the oven to 350°F/175°C.

2. In a small baking pan, toss the carrots in the olive oil and season with salt and pepper.

3. Roast until tender, 35 to 45 minutes. Set aside to cool. (If making ahead, refrigerate in an airtight container.)

MAKE THE ONIONS

1. Melt the butter in a large, heavy-bottomed skillet over medium-low heat. Add the onions and season with salt and pepper. Cover and cook until the onions release their liquid and begin to get soft, 10 to 12 minutes. Uncover, increase the heat to medium-high, and cook until the liquid evaporates and the onions turn golden brown, 8 to 10 minutes.

2. Set aside to cool. (If making ahead, refrigerate in an airtight container.)

MAKE THE POTATOES

1. Put the potatoes in a large pot, cover with cold water, and bring to a boil. Turn the heat down and simmer until the potatoes are tender but not falling apart. Drain.

2. When cool enough to handle, peel the potatoes, then pass them through a food mill or ricer into a straight-sided saucepan.

3. Heat the potatoes over medium heat, whipping with a stiff spoon or spatula to dry out the potatoes. While stirring, add the soft butter, a dab at a time, waiting until each is incorporated before adding the next, then the warm cream in a slow, steady stream. Season with salt and pepper and stir to combine. Set aside to cool. (If making ahead, refrigerate in an airtight container.)

MAKE THE SPINACH

1. Pour about ¼ inch/6 millimeters water into a medium pot. Heat the water over high heat, then add the spinach and toss with tongs. Cover and cook for 1 minute, then uncover and toss the spinach so that it all starts to wilt. Cover again and finish wilting, another minute or so. Remove from the heat, uncover, and let rest until it's cool enough to handle.

2. Wring out the spinach and set it aside. (If making ahead, refrigerate in an airtight container.)

FINISH THE PIE

1. Preheat the oven to 400°F/205°C.

2. Trim the cooled meat into two 2 by 5-inch/5 by 13-centimeter rectangles about ½ inch/1.25 centimeters thick. Lay out the meat slabs on a large platter or rimmed baking sheet.

3. Cut the carrots in half lengthwise. Place them cut side down on top of the meat. Trim the carrots to the size of the meat. Spread the potato over the carrots, pressing the potato down to fill the cracks.

4. Top with a layer of caramelized onions, then spinach. Coat with a few tablespoons of the reserved thickened braising liquid. Cover and refrigerate while you roll out the dough.

5. Roll the dough into a rectangle 16 inches/40 centimeters long, 10 inches/25 centimeters wide, and ⅛ inch/3 millimeters thick. Cut the rectangle in half so that you have two equal pieces.

6. For each pie, place a meat slab on one half of a piece of dough, vegetable side down. Egg wash the three edges of the dough around the meat, then fold the dough over the meat. Crimp to seal the three edges. Egg wash the top, refrigerate for 15 minutes, and egg wash again.

7. Bake until the crust is golden brown and the filling is hot all the way through, 25 to 30 minutes. Let rest for 5 to 10 minutes. Reheat the thickened braising liquid in a medium saucepan over medium-high heat. Serve the pies with the sauce.

SERVES 4

TURNOVERS

Michigan Upper Peninsula Pasties	155
Cornish-Style Pasties	156
Curried Duck or Chicken Turnovers	158
Curried Chickpea Turnovers	159
Roasted Curried Cauliflower Turnovers	160
Mom's Pierogis	162

The finished **Cornish-Style Pasty** (page 156), accompanied by a simple green salad

Turnovers are the easiest kinds of pie to make. One piece of dough is folded over to enclose a scoop of filling. Done. If the ingredients get wrapped in the dough raw, as they are with the Cornish pasty, it's even easier. Because the dough is a prominent part of the dish, it should be rich and delicious on its own, so we like to use the standard 3-2-1 Pie Dough or the Pâte Brisée. We're also including a pierogi recipe as it's a dough wrapped around a filling, just like a turnover, and it's a personal one for Brian, as he'll explain.

Michigan Upper Peninsula Pasties

This hand pie is a staple in the Upper Peninsula of Michigan, thought to have originated when immigrant miners arrived in this part of the country from Great Britain. Variations of these handheld pies are found in just about every diner from one end of Lake Superior to the other. It's the American version of the Cornish pasty, using a combination of ground beef and pork, with similar vegetables and aromatics.

- 8 ounces/225 grams ground beef
- 8 ounces/225 grams ground pork
- ¼ cup/30 grams minced onion
- ¼ cup/30 grams small-diced carrot
- ½ cup/60 grams small-diced russet potato
- ½ cup/60 grams small-diced rutabaga
- ¼ cup/14 grams minced fresh flat-leaf parsley
- 1 tablespoon fresh thyme leaves
  Kosher salt and freshly ground black pepper to taste
- 2 pounds/900 grams 3-2-1 Pie Dough (page 33)
  Egg Wash (page 28)

1. Preheat the oven to 350°F/175°C.

2. Combine the beef, pork, onion, carrot, potato, rutabaga, parsley, and thyme in a large bowl. Season with salt and pepper. Mix it all thoroughly by hand using a tiger claw method (stiffen your fingers into a claw), the more vigorously the better. Cook a tablespoon of the mixture in a small pan, taste, and adjust the seasoning as necessary.

3. Roll out the dough to ¼ inch/6 millimeters thick and cut out six 8-inch/20-centimeter circles.

4. Divide the filling mixture evenly among the dough circles, placing it on one half of the circle.

5. Egg wash one edge of each dough circle and fold over the filling into a half-moon shape. Starting at one end, roll the edges to crimp and seal the filling in the dough. Brush the top with egg wash, refrigerate for 15 minutes, and egg wash again. With a pair of scissors, cut three slits in the top.

6. Place the pasties on a rimmed baking sheet. Bake for 40 to 50 minutes, until the top is golden brown and the interior registers 150°F/65°C.

MAKES 6 PASTIES

Cornish-Style Pasties

If there is any recipe that exemplifies how simple and delicious making and eating a savory pie can be, this is it. These are served all over England but were originally linked to the town of Cornwall, where their name is protected. Pasties, so named for the paste they were wrapped in, have been made for centuries, but they became associated with Cornwall because they were a common lunch for the miners, who could carry this lunch in their pocket. The crust kept the ingredients from getting dirty and the pies could be heated on a shovel held over a fire.

It's preferable to make your own dough because store-bought dough just doesn't have enough butter in it and so doesn't make a good pasty. Of course, if you do choose to use store-bought pie dough, this preparation takes all of about 20 minutes to prepare.

The ingredients are seasoned, tossed, and placed raw on a disk of dough, which is then simply folded over the ingredients and baked. And it's a versatile preparation: Michael made these recently but, finding he had no fresh herbs, he seasoned the mixture with smoked paprika, cumin, and lots of black pepper and it was outstanding. Pasties can be eaten cold, but they smell so good coming out of the oven, you may not be able to help yourself from eating them straightaway. They can be made ahead and, when raw, freeze well.

⅓ cup/40 grams small-diced sweet onion
⅓ cup/40 grams small-diced carrot
⅓ cup/40 grams small-diced russet potato
⅓ cup/40 grams small-diced rutabaga
¼ cup/14 grams minced fresh flat-leaf parsley
1 tablespoon fresh thyme leaves
1½ pounds/680 grams 3-2-1 Pie Dough (page 33)
1 pound/450 grams beef skirt steak or other moderately tender cut, fat and sinew removed, cut into small dice
Kosher salt and freshly ground black pepper to taste
Egg Wash (page 28)

1. Preheat the oven to 350°F/175°C.

2. Combine the onion, carrot, potato, rutabaga, parsley, and thyme in a medium bowl and toss.

3. Roll out the dough ¼ inch/6 millimeters thick and cut out six 8-inch/20-centimeter circles.

4. Divide the vegetables among the dough circles, placing them on one half of the circle. Divide the meat evenly on top of the vegetables so that the juices will drip and coat the vegetables. Season with salt and pepper.

5. Egg wash one edge of each dough circle and fold over the filling to make a half-moon shape. Starting at one end, roll the edges to crimp and seal the filling in the dough. Brush the top with egg wash, refrigerate for 15 minutes, and egg wash again.

6. Place the pasties on a rimmed baking sheet. Bake for 40 to 50 minutes, until the top is golden brown and the filling is cooked through.

MAKES 6 PASTIES

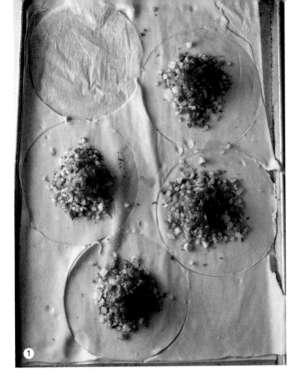

① In the Cornish pasty, all the ingredients are enclosed raw inside the dough. Notice that the vegetables are cut into small dice so that they cook evenly with the meat.

② Half the circle of dough is painted with egg wash for sealing. This pie uses what we call a ribbon crimp. Simply fold the dough over your thumb along the entire seam.

③ These are now ready to egg wash twice, then bake.

④ Cornish pasties can be eaten hot or at room temperature.

Curried Duck or Chicken Turnovers

Crust is a great vehicle for leftover roasted meats. When Brian was chef at the Lark, he often had duck on the menu. If he sold only seven of the eight ducks he'd prepared, he could pick the meat from the last one and turn it into a pie. Chicken works well here too, although duck is richer and more flavorful. The curry, cashews, and apple are classic pairings for either meat. These turnovers are fabulous for a light meal, or you can use the same filling mixture to make tiny turnovers and serve them as hors d'oeuvres.

 8 ounces/225 grams cooked roast duck or chicken meat, cartilage and sinew removed, cut into small dice
 ¼ cup/25 grams peeled, small-diced Granny Smith apple
 ¼ cup/25 grams chopped toasted cashews
 ¼ cup/14 grams thinly sliced scallions
 1½ teaspoons minced garlic
 2 tablespoons mayonnaise
 2 tablespoons curry powder
  Kosher salt and freshly ground black pepper to taste
 10 ounces/280 grams 3-2-1 Pie Dough (page 33)
  Egg Wash (page 28)

1. Preheat the oven to 350°F/175°C.

2. Combine the duck, apple, cashews, scallions, garlic, mayonnaise, and curry power in a large bowl and mix thoroughly. Taste and season with salt and pepper as necessary.

3. Roll out the dough ⅛ inch/3 millimeters thick and cut out eight 4-inch/10-centimeter circles.

4. Divide the filling mixture evenly among the eight circles, placing it on one half of the circle. Egg wash one edge of each dough circle and fold over the filling into a half-moon shape. Starting at one end, roll the edges to crimp and seal the filling in the dough. Brush the top with egg wash, refrigerate for 15 minutes, and egg wash again.

5. Place the turnovers on a rimmed baking sheet. Bake for 25 to 30 minutes, until the top is golden brown.

MAKES 8 TURNOVERS

Curried Chickpea Turnovers

Our editor, Melanie Tortoroli, hinted that she'd love to see something with chickpeas and curry—they make a perfect turnover filling—so this one is for her. It's very simple—just make sure to use a good red Thai curry paste, not powdered. If you start with dried chickpeas, and this is ideal, be sure to cook them thoroughly, until quite tender. But canned chickpeas work too.

1 tablespoon olive oil
¼ cup/42 grams thinly sliced onion
1 tablespoon grated fresh ginger
1 tablespoon red Thai curry paste
2 tablespoons sweetened coconut milk
1 cup/166 grams cooked or canned chickpeas
2 tablespoons chopped fresh cilantro
   Kosher salt and freshly ground black pepper
   to taste
8 ounces/225 grams Pâte Brisée (page 33)
   Egg Wash (page 28)

1. Preheat the oven to 375°F/190°C.

2. Heat the oil in a large saucepan over medium heat. When the oil is hot, add the onion and ginger and cook just until the onion is tender but not browned, 6 to 8 minutes. Add the curry paste and stir well to cook it for 20 seconds or so. Add the coconut milk, chickpeas, and cilantro, then season with salt and pepper. Set aside to cool.

3. Transfer the mixture to a food processor and puree until you achieve the consistency you like—anywhere from chunky to coarse to smooth like hummus.

4. On a floured surface, roll out the dough to ⅛ inch/3 millimeters thick. Using a 3½-inch/9-centimeter round biscuit cutter, cut out 12 circles.

5. Spoon about 2 tablespoons of the chickpea mixture onto half of each dough circle. Egg wash one edge of each dough circle and fold over the filling into a half-moon shape. Starting at one end, roll the edges to crimp and seal the filling in the dough. Egg wash the top, refrigerate for 15 minutes, and egg wash again.

6. Place the turnovers on a rimmed baking sheet. Bake for 12 to 15 minutes, until golden brown and cooked through.

MAKES 12 TURNOVERS

Roasted Curried Cauliflower Turnovers

Curry and cauliflower are an unbeatable pair in this vegetarian handheld pie. Roasting the cauliflower until it is beautifully browned adds deeply satisfying flavor, and mayonnaise adds moisture. We prefer Madras curry powder for this recipe, but you can use any type you like as long as it is fresh. A lot of people use spices that have been sitting too long on their spice rack or in a drawer and have lost most of their flavor. A good rule of thumb for all your spices is this: If you don't remember when you bought it, it's probably time to buy a fresh tin or jar.

- 1 head cauliflower (2 to 2½ pounds/900 to 1125 grams), trimmed and broken into small florets
- 3 tablespoons olive oil
  Kosher salt and freshly ground black pepper to taste
- ¾ cup/112 grams small-diced onion
- 1 tablespoon minced garlic
- 2 tablespoons Madras curry powder or curry powder of your choice
- 3 tablespoons mayonnaise
- 1½ pounds/680 grams 3-2-1 Pie Dough (page 33)
  Egg Wash (page 28)

1. Preheat the oven to 350°F/175°C. Line a rimmed baking sheet with parchment paper.

2. Spread out the cauliflower florets in a single layer on the lined baking sheet. Drizzle with 2 tablespoons olive oil and season with salt and pepper. Bake until golden brown, about 30 minutes. Cool to room temperature. Leave the oven on.

3. Meanwhile, heat the remaining 1 tablespoon olive oil in a large sauté pan over medium heat. When the oil is hot, add the onion and garlic and sauté until soft but not browned, 6 to 8 minutes. Add 1 tablespoon curry powder, season with salt and pepper, and stir, then cool to room temperature.

4. Roll out the dough ⅛ inch/3 millimeters thick. Using a 4-inch/10-centimeter round biscuit cutter, measure the dough to ensure you can fit 12 circles. If you can't, roll out the dough a little thinner. Cut out 12 circles.

5. Break the cauliflower into very small pieces into a large bowl and add the onion mixture, mayonnaise, and remaining 1 tablespoon curry powder. Season with salt and pepper.

6. Spoon about 2 tablespoons of the cauliflower mixture onto half of each dough circle. Egg wash one edge of each dough circle and fold over the filling into a half-moon shape. Starting at one end, roll the edges to crimp and seal the filling in the dough. Egg wash the top, refrigerate for 15 minutes, and egg wash again.

7. Place the turnovers on a rimmed baking sheet. Bake for about 30 minutes, until golden brown.

MAKES 12 TURNOVERS

Everyone loves these flaky, spicy, curried **cauliflower mini pies**. Brian brought them to the last Super Bowl party he went to—they're an unusual and flavorful offering and always disappear fast. Notice how the stuffing is popping out of the turnover. This happened because the young chef making them for Chef Brian failed to seal them thoroughly with egg wash. Brian prefers them fully closed and crimped. But our photographer, Quentin Bacon, loved the openings so much, he convinced Brian to let him shoot these. Now we love them this way, too!

Mom's Pierogis

Here's Brian on this family recipe:

These are really important to me because the recipe comes from my mom, who died at age 96, while Michael and I were working on this book. She was Mexican and my dad was Polish. A few years ago she asked me to help her write an accurate recipe for these pierogis that she could give to her fifteen grandchildren—she wanted her cooking to be passed down to them. I went to her house with a notebook and she got to work.

"First," she said, reaching into the flour container, "you put five handfuls of flour in the—"

"Ma, wait. You can't do that. The kids all have different hand sizes."

I live nearby, so I ran home for my scale.

"OK," I said, "you measure as you normally do, and I'll weight it."

And in this way we recreated her pierogi recipe for her grandchildren, and now for this book.

These are simple, traditional pierogis, kind of like a boiled turnover. They're filled with fresh cheese and blanched until the dough is cooked, then reheated in butter. Mom always served these simply with sour cream.

Miss you, Ma.

FOR THE DOUGH

- 2 large eggs plus 6 large egg yolks
- ¼ cup/60 milliliters olive oil
- ¼ cup/60 milliliters whole milk
- 2⅓ cups/285 grams all-purpose flour
- 1 teaspoon/5 grams kosher salt

FOR THE FILLING

- 2 pounds/900 grams farmers cheese
- 2 large eggs plus 1 large egg yolk
- 1 teaspoon kosher salt

TO SERVE

Unsalted butter, for sautéing

1. Combine all of the dough ingredients in a food processor and pulse until it binds. Remove the dough from the processor and wrap in plastic. Let rest on the counter for 30 minutes, while you make the filling.

2. Clean the food processor. Combine all of the filling ingredients in the food processor and process until smooth.

3. Divide the dough into three equal pieces. Roll out the first piece ⅛ inch/3 millimeters thick. Using a 5-inch/13-centimeter round biscuit cutter, measure to ensure you can fit 12 circles. If you can't, roll out the dough a little thinner. Cut out 12 circles. Repeat with the remaining dough.

4. Divide the filling mixture evenly onto the dough circles. Fold over and crimp with a fork.

5. Bring a large pot of water to a boil. Working in batches, poach the pierogis just until the dough is set, 3 to 5 minutes. Transfer to a rimmed baking sheet lined with paper towels. (At this point the pierogis can be cooled and stored on a sheet tray lined with plastic wrap, the pierogis covered with plastic wrap, in the freezer for up to 3 months. Thaw before sautéing in butter.)

6. To serve, melt plenty of butter in a large skillet over medium-high heat. Sauté the pierogis until lightly browned on both sides and hot in the middle, 6 to 8 minutes. Serve right away.

MAKES 36 PIEROGIS

"Sour cream and chives are a must," Brian says. "You cannot have my mother's pierogis without sour cream. She worked on this recipe for thirty-five years, always trying to make it better. She made them in batches of thirty-six; that was her formula. Several years ago, she and I wrote down the recipe that she did from memory and feel. At Christmas she gave thirty-four grandchildren and great-grandchildren this recipe and a marble rolling pin. That's why these pierogis are so important to me. She inspired me to be a chef."

VOL-AU-VENTS

Vol-au-Vent Pastry Shells   168

Escargots with Parsley and Garlic
    Vol-au-Vents   170

Sautéed Gulf Shrimp with Cognac and
    Cream Vol-au-Vents   172

Creamed Morel and Asparagus   173

Crawfish and Andouille
    Vol-au-Vents   175

Seared Sea Scallop with Sweet Corn and
    Roasted Red Pepper Vol-au-Vents   176

Emincé of Chicken with Lemon,
    Tarragon, and Garlic Vol-au-Vents   177

These mini tarts are the easiest preparation in the entire pie repertoire to serve. Once the shell is baked, you simply fill it and you're done. And as with most pies, they're easy to make ahead of time. They're also really fun to eat. And they can be filled with virtually anything you wish. In this chapter we offer six delicious fillings for vol-au-vents.

Vol-au-vents literally translates from the French as "windblown," for the light-as-air texture of the puff pastry. We like to use our Blitz Puff Pastry Dough (page 36), but it's perfectly fine to use store-bought puff pastry, which is sold not only in sheets but also in preshaped vol-au-vents. Frozen puff pastry is typically made with vegetable shortening, so the dough isn't as flavorful or rich as a dough you make with butter and cream. But for convenience, store-bought can't be beat.

The pastry shells can be made the size of a dinner plate, if you wanted, but most often you'll see vol-au-vents either bite-size (known as bouchées) or 3 to 4 inches/7.5 to 10 centimeters across to be part of a main dish or even the main dish itself.

Here are some rules to live by when working with puff pastry:

- Proper temperature of the dough is critical. It needs to stay cold so that you don't lose the distinct layers of butter and dough. The dough must be chilled before rolling and cutting, and again before baking.

- Don't roll the dough in one direction; instead, roll right to left and then up and down. This prevents your round shells from turning into ovals.

- When cutting the dough, use a very sharp knife or biscuit cutter to avoid mashing the laminated layers together, as this will inhibit lift.

- Be careful when you brush on the egg wash, especially on the tops. If the wash runs down the sides and dries there, if can prevent that area from rising.

- Use a flat, heavy-gauge baking sheet that is not warped when baking puff pastry (or anything, really—those wobbly, buckling cookie sheets are not worth having).

- Vol-au-vents are almost always served hot. But you can often make the filling ahead of time and reheat it over medium-low heat just before filling the pastry shells. Once filled, they should be served immediately.

Vol-au-Vent Pastry Shells

1 pound/450 grams Blitz Puff Pastry Dough
(page 36)
Egg Wash (page 28)

1. On a sheet of parchment paper, roll out the chilled dough to ¼ inch/6 millimeters thick. With a 3½-inch/9-centimeter round biscuit cutter, cut out eight circles. With a 3-inch/7.5-centimeter ring cutter or a paring knife, cut out the center of each circle, leaving a ½-inch/1.25-centimeter ring. Refrigerate the rings on the lined baking sheet. Reserve all of the cut-out middles and trimmings.

2. Reroll the middles and trimmings to ⅛ inch/3 millimeters thick and chill. Cut out eight 3½-inch/9-centimeter circles for the bases. Place on the lined rimmed baking sheet. With a fork, poke holes in the bases, then egg wash them and refrigerate.

3. Preheat the oven to 450°F/230°C.

4. Carefully place a dough ring on top of each base. Egg wash the tops, making sure it doesn't drip down the sides. Chill completely.

5. Place a 1-inch/2.5-centimeter aluminum foil ball in each corner of the rimmed baking sheet. (If you use pieces of foil that are the same size, your foil balls will be similar in size.) Place a wire rack on top of the foil balls so it is suspended above the uncooked vol-au-vents. (This will ensure that they rise evenly; if they start to rise on an angle, they will hit the rack and stay even.)

6. Bake the vol-au-vents until they rise and turn golden, 12 to 15 minutes. Do not open the oven for the first 8 to 10 minutes.

7. Turn the oven temperature down to 350°F/175°C and allow them to finish baking, 20 to 25 minutes. They should be dry all the way through. Allow the pastry shells to cool.

8. The bottoms will have puffed up so, with a sharp paring knife, cut out the center of each to make a deep cup. Be careful not to poke all the way through the bottom.

9. The baked shells can be stored in an airtight container in a cool, dry place for up to 4 days, or frozen and then thawed. When ready to use, rebake at 325°F/160°C to crisp them up again before filling.

MAKES 8 VOL-AU-VENT PASTRY SHELLS

① To make four vol-au-vents, cut eight circles from your Blitz Puff Pastry Dough. First egg wash the circles, taking care to coat only the tops; egg wash that dribbles down the side can prevent those areas from rising properly. After egg washing, dock four of the circles and cut the centers out of the other four. (Note: Excess dough can be re-rolled and saved or used elsewhere, but it won't have the lift that the original dough has.)

② After placing the rings on top of the bases, set up a jig so that they rise to identical heights: Crumple balls of aluminum foil that are about 1 inch/2.5 centimeters in diameter. Set the balls in the corners of the pan and set a rack on the balls. The vol-au-vent shells can only rise to the level of the rack. (Be sure to put your rack upside down onto the foil balls if it has feet, as this one does.)

③ After they are baked, you'll see that the center of the base will have risen and browned. Using a paring or small serrated knife, cut this center piece out of all the shells.

Escargots *with Parsley and Garlic Vol-au-Vents*

This recipe goes back all the way to Brian's days at the Golden Mushroom in the mid-1980s. Because the dish can be made ahead of time, he would make a big batch at the beginning of the week, and whenever an order came up, it took about 60 seconds to add the snails, reheat the sauce, and fill the vol-au-vents. (This filling would also make terrific individual pot pies.)

The best snails are of the Helix genus, large land snails, and are commonly raised in Burgundy, France. They're available canned at most finer grocery stores and online.

   3 ounces/90 grams unsalted butter
¼ cup/50 grams minced garlic
   2 tablespoons minced shallot
¼ cup/60 milliliters dry white wine
¼ cup/60 milliliters chicken stock or canned clam juice
¼ cup cornstarch slurry (see page 46), or as needed
¼ cup/60 milliliters heavy cream
¼ cup/14 grams chopped fresh flat-leaf parsley
24 large Helix snails, drained
   Kosher salt and freshly ground black pepper to taste
   8 Vol-au-Vent Pastry Shells (page 168)

1. Melt the butter in a large, heavy-bottomed saucepan over medium heat. Add the garlic and shallot and sauté until soft but not browned, 3 to 4 minutes. Add the wine and stock and bring to a boil.

2. Gradually add the cornstarch slurry, stirring until the sauce is thickened, 1 to 2 minutes. Stir in the cream, then fold in the parsley.

3. Add the snails to the sauce and heat over medium-high heat until warmed through. Taste for seasoning, and add salt and pepper as necessary.

4. Fill the shells and serve.

MAKES 8 VOL-AU-VENTS

Vol-au-vents can be filled with anything thick and creamy. Here we have, clockwise from the top: **Emincé of Chicken with Lemon, Tarragon, and Garlic** (page 177), **Sautéed Gulf Shrimp with Cognac and Cream** (page 172), **Escargots with Parsley and Garlic** (this page), and **Crawfish and Andouille** (page 175).

Sautéed Gulf Shrimp *with Cognac and Cream Vol-au-Vents*

Cognac is a fabulous flavor pairing for shrimp, and the cream connects all the flavors. We use a little chicken stock, but if you have a lot of shrimp shells, you can make a shrimp stock: Sauté the shells in some butter with finely sliced onion and carrot, add a little tomato paste, deglaze with Cognac, cover with water, and simmer for 15 to 20 minutes, then strain.

- 1 ounce/30 grams unsalted butter
- 16 jumbo (16/20) shrimp (about 1 pound/450 grams), peeled and deveined
  Kosher salt and freshly ground black pepper to taste
- ¼ cup/60 milliliters Cognac or brandy
- 2 tablespoons chicken stock
- 1 tablespoon freshly squeezed lemon juice
- 1 teaspoon tomato paste
- ½ cup/120 milliliters heavy cream
- 2 tablespoons chopped fresh chives
- 8 Vol-au-Vent Pastry Shells (page 168)

1. Melt the butter in a large sauté pan over medium heat. Add the shrimp, season with salt and pepper, and cook until the shrimp start to turn pink, 3 to 4 minutes. Turn the heat up to high, add the Cognac, and carefully ignite the brandy to burn off the alcohol. Add the stock, lemon juice, and tomato paste and dissolve the tomato paste in the juices using the back of a spoon. Add the cream and bring to a simmer, then cook until the sauce is thick and the shrimp are cooked through, 4 to 6 minutes. Fold in the chives.

2. Put 2 shrimp in each shell, divide the sauce evenly between them, and serve.

MAKES 8 VOL-AU-VENTS

Creamed Morel and Asparagus Vol-au-Vents

This is a particularly delicious and common pairing in the spring, as the first shoots of green asparagus appear in tandem with the otherworldly-looking morel mushroom. Folk wisdom says that when you smell the lilacs, that's when to hunt for morels, which are one of the easiest wild mushrooms to identify. Happily, more and more supermarkets carry fresh morels when they're in season. They are especially flavorful in a cream sauce.

Kosher salt and freshly ground black pepper to taste
8 asparagus tips
1 ounce/30 grams unsalted butter
1 pound/450 grams morel mushrooms, cleaned and halved lengthwise
2 tablespoons minced shallot
½ cup/120 milliliters dry sherry
1 tablespoon all-purpose flour
¾ cup/180 milliliters heavy cream
2 tablespoons chopped fresh chives
8 Vol-au-Vent Pastry Shells (page 168)

1. Bring a small pot of salted water to a boil, add the asparagus tips, and blanch until tender, 4 to 5 minutes. Transfer to a large bowl of ice water to stop the cooking process, drain again, and set aside.

2. Melt the butter in a large skillet over medium heat. Add the morels and shallot and sauté until the mushrooms are heated through, 2 to 3 minutes. Add the sherry, turn the heat up to medium-high, and simmer until the liquid is almost gone, 4 to 5 minutes. Sprinkle the flour over the mushrooms and stir to incorporate. Add the cream and simmer until it thickens, 4 to 5 minutes. Season with salt and pepper. Fold in the chives.

3. Heat the asparagus tips in a separate pan with a little butter or microwave briefly to reheat.

4. Fill the shells with the creamed morels. Insert two asparagus tips in each vol-au-vent and serve.

MAKES 8 VOL-AU-VENTS

Crawfish and Andouille Vol-au-Vents

Crawfish (also known as crayfish) have a delectable sweetness that works great in a creamy sauce with another Creole/Cajun staple, andouille sausage. Frozen crawfish tails are available from the Louisiana Crawfish Company.

1 ounce/30 grams unsalted butter

¼ cup/30 grams small-diced green bell pepper

1 tablespoon minced garlic

4 ounces/112 grams smoked andouille sausage, cut about the same size as the crawfish meat

¾ cup/180 milliliters heavy cream

8 ounces/240 grams cooked crawfish tail meat
Kosher salt and freshly ground black pepper to taste

8 Vol-au-Vent Pastry Shells (page 168)

1. Melt the butter in a large skillet over medium heat. Add the green pepper and garlic and sauté until the pepper is soft, 4 to 5 minutes. Add the sausage and brown lightly. Add the cream, turn the heat up to medium-high, and simmer to reduce the cream until it's thick, 5 to 6 minutes. Fold in the crawfish and season with salt and pepper.

2. Fill the shells and serve.

MAKES 8 VOL-AU-VENTS

Pastry shells should be made ahead and will keep for up to 4 days in an airtight container. Always crisp up the shells in a 325°F/160°C oven for 4 or 5 minutes before filling. These shells overflow with **crawfish and andouille**.

Seared Sea Scallop
with Sweet Corn and Roasted Red Pepper Vol-au-Vents

Scallops and corn are as felicitous a pairing as morels and asparagus (see page 175). Here the corn is cooked and then pureed for a very creamy, corn-rich sauce that finishes the seared scallops. Roasted red peppers add color and more flavor. Don't cut the scallops too small; you want chunks that will just fit in the pastry cup.

1 red bell pepper
1 ounce/30 grams unsalted butter
  Corn kernels cut from 2 ears
  Kosher salt and freshly ground black pepper to taste
¾ cup/180 milliliters heavy cream
2 tablespoons olive oil
1 pound/450 grams fresh sea scallops, cut into medium dice
3 tablespoons chopped fresh chives
8 Vol-au-Vent Pastry Shells (page 168)

1. Roast the bell pepper over an open flame until the skin turns black and blisters. (Alternatively, you can cut the pepper in half and broil until blackened.) Put the pepper in a bowl and cover tightly with plastic wrap. When cool, remove the charred skin and seeds. Cut the pepper into small dice and set aside.

2. Melt the butter in a large, heavy-bottomed sauté pan over medium heat. Add the corn, season with salt and pepper, cover, and cook until the corn is heated through, a few minutes. Add the cream and bring it to a simmer, then remove the pan from the heat.

3. Transfer the mixture to a blender. Remove the center of the blender lid and cover the hole with a kitchen towel to allow steam to escape, then puree until smooth.

4. Heat the oil in a large sauté pan over high heat. When the oil is hot, add the scallops and sear on both sides until they are browned and just translucent, 1 to 2 minutes. Hold a strainer over the scallops and pour in the corn sauce from the blender. When the sauce is hot, turn the heat down to low and fold in the chives and roasted red pepper.

5. Fill the shells and serve.

MAKES 8 VOL-AU-VENTS

Emincé of Chicken
with Lemon, Tarragon, and Garlic Vol-au-Vents

Emincé is a French term meaning cut into thin strips. Since the meat will be quickly sautéed, it's important to use a tender muscle, such as chicken breast. This cream sauce would also be a good way to use trim from lean white fish. Simply add 8 ounces/225 grams fish trimmings when the sauce is finishing and cook until heated through. If using fish, it's ideal to use a fish stock, but not mandatory.

8 ounces/225 grams boneless, skinless chicken breast, cut into 1 inch by ½-inch/2.5 by 1.25-centimeter slices, about ¼ inch/6 millimeters thick
Kosher salt and freshly ground black pepper to taste
1 ounce/30 grams unsalted butter
1 tablespoon minced garlic
3 tablespoons dry white wine
Juice of 1 lemon
¾ cup/180 milliliters chicken stock
¼ cup cornstarch slurry (see page 46), or as needed
3 tablespoons chopped fresh tarragon
8 Vol-au-Vent Pastry Shells (page 168)

1. Season the chicken with salt and pepper. Melt the butter in a large skillet over medium-high heat. Working in batches, add the chicken and brown for 2 to 3 minutes, being careful not to let it burn. Transfer the chicken to a plate.

2. Add the garlic and stir to cook it for 30 seconds or so. Deglaze the pan with the wine and lemon juice and let it cook until reduced by three-quarters, 4 to 5 minutes. Add the stock and bring it to simmer. Taste for seasoning, and add salt and pepper as necessary.

3. Gradually add the cornstarch slurry to the simmering stock, stirring until the sauce is thickened, 1 to 2 minutes.

4. Return the chicken to the pan and turn the heat down to medium-low. Fold in the tarragon.

5. Fill the shells and serve.

MAKES 8 VOL-AU-VENTS

Roasted New Potato and Scallion Salad (page 181)

Cucumber and Smoked Ham Salad (page 183)

Honey Garlic Roasted Carrots (page 182)

Carrot and Parsnip Mash (page 185)

III

✳

SIDES
FOR
PIES

Roasted New Potato and Scallion Salad   181

Brian's Mashed Potatoes   181

Potato and Garlic Puree   182

Honey-Garlic Roasted Carrots   182

Cucumber and Smoked Ham Salad   183

Apple, Cabbage, and Blue Cheese Slaw   183

Shaved Fennel and Red Onion Salad   184

Quick-Pickled Red Cabbage   184

Roasted Beets with Arugula or Watercress   185

Carrot and Parsnip Mash   185

The classic combination for a meat pie is a side of mashed potatoes, gravy, and peas. Nothing wrong with that at all. But pies can be so many things, from a center-of-the-plate featured dish to an accompaniment to another dish to a luncheon item to an hors d'oeuvres. To encourage you to make and enjoy a variety of pies, Brian has created ten all-purpose sides that will go with any pie in the book. (Frankly, they're all great side dishes period, whether they're served with pie or not.)

Roasted New Potato and Scallion Salad

Simple as promised: new potatoes roasted with olive oil, cooled, and tossed with mustard.

12 ounces/340 grams new potatoes, well scrubbed
1 tablespoon olive oil
1½ tablespoons Dijon mustard
2 scallions, sliced feather-thin on the bias
Kosher salt and freshly ground black pepper to taste

1. Preheat the oven to 350°F/175°C. Line a rimmed baking sheet with parchment paper.

2. On the lined baking sheet, toss the potatoes with the olive oil. Roast until tender, about 35 minutes. Allow to cool to room temperature.

3. Cut the potatoes into bite-size pieces (quarters if they're big, halves if they're small). Put them in a large bowl, add the mustard and scallions, season with salt and pepper, and toss well.

SERVES 4

Brian's Mashed Potatoes

There are a lot of ways to make pureed potatoes, the most famous of which is from the late uber-chef Joël Robuchon, who used as much butter as he did potato. The mashed many of us grew up on were lumpy but delicious. This recipe is kind of an all-purpose potato puree.

The important thing when choosing potatoes is the starch content. For a rich, creamy, mashed potato, not a starchy, gluey one, you'll want to use russets, or baking potatoes. To remove excess starch, peel and dice the potatoes and rinse them under cold water before cooking.

2 pounds/900 grams russet potatoes, peeled and cut into 1-inch/2.5-centimeter dice
½ cup/120 milliliters whole milk or heavy cream, warmed
4 ounces/115 grams unsalted butter, melted
Kosher salt and freshly ground black pepper to taste

1. Rinse the potatoes under cold water.

2. Put the potatoes in a large pot, cover with cold water, and bring to a simmer. Cook the potatoes until completely tender, 10 to 12 minutes, without letting the water reach a boil. Drain and let the potatoes steam off for several minutes, then dry them on a kitchen towel.

3. For the smoothest puree, push the potatoes through a ricer or food mill; otherwise mash using a potato masher.

4. Stirring continuously, add the warm milk and melted butter until they are incorporated. Season with salt and pepper.

SERVES 6

Potato and Garlic Puree

This version of mashed potatoes is excellent with all vegetable pies, hot or cold. Pureed potatoes are neutral in taste and accept other flavors while adding depth to the meal. Here the potatoes are flavored with garlic minced to a paste, olive oil, and some lemon juice.

- 1 pound/450 grams russet potatoes, well scrubbed
- 6 garlic cloves, peeled
- 2 tablespoons freshly squeezed lemon juice
  Kosher salt and freshly ground black pepper to taste
- ¼ cup/60 milliliters olive oil

1. Put the potatoes in a large pot, cover with cold water, and bring to a simmer. Cook the potatoes until completely tender but before the skin splits, 15 to 18 minutes, without letting the water reach a boil. Drain.

2. When cool enough to handle, peel the potatoes and cut into 1-inch/2.5-centimeter pieces.

3. While the potatoes are cooking, mash the garlic cloves with the flat side of a chef's knife on a cutting board. Mince the garlic, occasionally smearing it against the cutting board, until it becomes a fine paste.

4. Put the potatoes and garlic in a food processor, add the lemon juice, and season with salt and pepper. Pulse a couple of times to puree the potatoes, then drizzle in the olive oil with the motor running until well incorporated. If the puree is too thick, you can add a little more olive oil, but not too much or else the potatoes will have a greasy or broken texture. You can also thin it out with a little hot chicken stock.

SERVES 4

Honey-Garlic Roasted Carrots

In this simple preparation, carrots are tossed with flavorful oil, garlic, honey, and parsley and roasted. Buy bunch carrots (carrots with their stems still attached) rather than bagged carrots. Or use multicolored carrots.

- 12 ounces/340 grams carrots (about 1 inch/2.5 centimeters in diameter), peeled
- 2 tablespoons olive oil
  Kosher salt and freshly ground black pepper
- 1½ teaspoons minced garlic
- 2 tablespoons honey
- 1 tablespoon minced fresh flat-leaf parsley

1. Preheat the oven to 350°F/175°C.

2. On a rimmed baking sheet, toss the carrots with the olive oil and season with salt and pepper. Roast until tender, about 25 minutes.

3. Combine the garlic and honey in a large bowl. Add the hot carrots and toss to coat evenly. Top with the parsley.

SERVES 4

Cucumber and Smoked Ham Salad

This is a simple salad with no cooking required: cukes, ham, sour cream, and vinegar. Hearty but refreshing.

- 1 English cucumber
  Kosher salt to taste
- 3 ounces/90 grams smoked ham, julienned
- 3 tablespoons sour cream
- 1 tablespoon red wine vinegar
- 1 tablespoon chopped fresh flat-leaf parsley

1. Peel the cucumber, then quarter it lengthwise. Scoop out the seeds, then cut the cucumber into ½-inch/1.25-centimeter pieces on the bias. Sprinkle with salt and lay out on paper towels to drain.

2. Pat the cucumbers dry and put them in a medium bowl. Add the ham, sour cream, vinegar, and parsley and toss to combine.

SERVES 4

Apple, Cabbage, and Blue Cheese Slaw

This slaw is particularly good with the hand-raised pies. Blue cheese makes it a standout.

- 8 ounces/225 grams green cabbage (about ¼ head), cut into a fine julienne
- 1 Honeycrisp apple, peeled, cored, and cut into thin strips or julienned
- 3 scallions, sliced feather-thin on the bias
- ¼ cup/60 milliliters olive oil
- 1 tablespoon red wine vinegar
- 4 ounces/115 grams blue cheese, crumbled

1. Combine all of the ingredients in a large bowl and toss well.

SERVES 4

Shaved Fennel and Red Onion Salad

The key to this simple salad, seasoned with nothing more than olive oil, salt, and pepper, is slicing the vegetables as thinly as possible. A Japanese mandoline is ideal for this, but a very sharp knife will work as well.

- ½ red onion, shaved or very thinly sliced (about ⅓ cup/40 grams)
  Kosher salt and freshly ground black pepper to taste
- 1 large fennel bulb, fronds removed and reserved, bulb shaved or very thinly sliced (about 1 cup/115 grams)
- 2 to 3 tablespoons olive oil

1. If you would like to soften the sharp taste of the onion, salt it generously, let it sit for 10 minutes, then rinse well. Drain and pat dry with paper towels.

2. In a large bowl, combine the onion, fennel, fennel fronds, and olive oil and toss well. Season with salt and pepper.

SERVES 4

Quick-Pickled Red Cabbage

Traditional sauerkraut takes at least a week to make. This recipe doesn't take long to throw together, but it does require sitting overnight, so make this at least a day before serving (it will keep for a month in the refrigerator). If you want to make only half a batch, use half a cabbage, but keep the amounts of the remaining ingredients the same.

- 1 (1-pound/450-gram) red cabbage, cored and shredded or julienned
- ¾ cup/180 milliliters water
- ¾ cup/180 milliliters cider vinegar
- 1 garlic clove, thinly sliced
- 1 teaspoon coriander seeds
- 6 whole black peppercorns
- 1 teaspoon kosher salt
- 1 teaspoon sugar

1. Put the cabbage in a large glass jar or plastic container.

2. Combine the water, vinegar, garlic, coriander seeds, peppercorns, salt, and sugar in a small saucepan and bring to a simmer. Pour the mixture over the cabbage. Cover and refrigerate overnight before serving.

SERVES 6 TO 8

Roasted Beets with Arugula or Watercress

Roasted beets with peppery greens is an easy, delicious, and nutritious side dish. Make this in spring when a variety of yellow and red beets come into season.

   12 ounces/360 grams small beets
    3 tablespoons olive oil
    2 cups/80 grams watercress or arugula
       Kosher salt and freshly ground black pepper
       to taste

1. Preheat the oven to 350°F/175°C.

2. Toss the beets with 1 tablespoon olive oil, wrap them in aluminum foil, and place in a small baking pan. Roast until tender, about 45 minutes, then cool to room temperature.

3. Rub the skins off the beets, then cut them into thin wedges. In a medium bowl, toss the beets with 1 tablespoon olive oil and season with salt and pepper.

4. In a large bowl, toss the greens with the remaining 1 tablespoon olive oil and season with salt and pepper.

5. Add the beets to the greens and toss well.

SERVES 4

Carrot and Parsnip Mash

If you want to go beyond mashed potatoes, try this root vegetable mash. Like mashed potatoes, this goes especially well with double-crusted and rolled raised pies.

       Kosher salt and freshly ground black pepper
       to taste
    8 ounces/225 grams carrots, peeled and cut into
       1-inch/2.5-centimeter dice
    8 ounces/225 grams parsnips, peeled and cut
       into 1-inch/2.5-centimeter dice
    1 tablespoon olive oil
    2 ounces/60 grams unsalted butter, softened
    1 tablespoon minced fresh flat-leaf parsley

1. Fill two small saucepans with water, generously season with salt, and bring to a simmer. Add the carrots to one pan and the parsnips to the other pan and simmer until tender, 10 to 15 minutes (they cook differently). Drain them and let them steam off for a few minutes.

2. Combine the carrots and parsnips in a bowl, add the oil and butter, and mash with a potato masher or the back of a fork. They should be somewhat lumpy. Season to taste with salt and pepper, then fold in the parsley.

SERVES 4

Hot Mustard #1 (page 191)

Hot Mustard #2 (page 191)

Faux French's Yellow American Mustard (page 191)

Mustard-Horseradish-Dill Sauce (page 194)

IV

SAUCES AND CONDIMENTS

Chicken Stock	189
Easy Overnight Chicken Stock	189
Hot Mustard #1	191
Hot Mustard #2	191
Faux French's Yellow American Mustard	191
All-Purpose Gravy	192
Red Currant Sauce	193
Mustard-Horseradish-Dill Sauce	194
Apple Horseradish	194
Apple Horseradish Mayonnaise	195
Sweet Onion Sauce	195
Mushroom Jus Lié	196
Apricot and Sweet Onion Chutney	196
Red Onion Relish	197
Roasted Red Pepper Relish	197

Not every pie needs a sauce or a condiment, but many are elevated by them. When we wrote *Charcuterie,* we announced, "Sauces and condiments: *not* optional." Virtually every preparation in that book benefited from some kind of sauce, which introduced moisture, flavor, and texture. "Most chefs worth their salt," we wrote, "would as willingly enter the dining room naked as send a dish to a customer without a sauce." This remains true. But, in the case of the savory pie, it doesn't necessarily go on the side. Many pies come with their own sauce baked right in. All the pot pies are, in effect, stews topped with a crust—the braising liquid is the sauce. If your pot pie needs a sauce, you probably didn't make it right!

But meat-heavy preparations, such as the American Pekin Duck Pie with Pistachios (page 134), definitely benefit from a sauce in the same way a pâté en croûte does—a red currant sauce, for instance, or our apple horseradish, or even a chutney. Most two-crusted pies benefit from a sauce; the Chicken Sheet Pan Pie (page 140) is delicious on its own, but give a finished piece a small ladle of mushroom jus lié, and you have elevated the dish immeasurably.

Happily, whether to offer a sauce with a dish or not is determined in large part by common sense. It should be obvious that you wouldn't serve a sausage roll or pork pie with a creamy dill sauce—you'd save that sauce for coulibiac, the Atlantic Salmon in Puff Pastry (page 144)—and put a little Dijon or Colman's mustard on the pork. The Stilton Cheesecake with Walnut Crust (page 119) is even more delicious if you serve a red currant sauce with it.

To reiterate, not all pies need a sauce, but some, while fine on their own, become a much more satisfying dish to eat when sauced.

Chicken Stock

This is an excellent, all-purpose chicken stock, and can be used for cooking or thickened for gravy. It uses uncooked chicken bones, so it's important to skim diligently as the water comes to a simmer. Cook at the lowest possible heat, just below a simmer, with one or two bubbles coming to the surface every now and then. This will help keep the stock clear.

- 8 pounds/3.6 kilograms raw chicken bones, necks, feet, and giblets
- 1 cup/150 grams roughly chopped onion
- ½ cup/75 grams roughly chopped celery
- ½ cup/75 grams roughly chopped carrot
- 2 bay leaves
- 10 whole black peppercorns, cracked with the side of a knife or a sauté pan
  About 6 quarts/6 liters cold water

1. Combine the chicken parts, onion, celery, carrot, bay leaves, and cracked peppercorns in a large pot that is taller than it is wide. Add the water; it should cover the ingredients by about 1 inch/2.5 centimeters. Bring the water to a simmer, skimming as you do. Turn the heat down so that the pot is just below a simmer and cook, skimming occasionally, for 5 hours.

2. Strain through a fine-mesh sieve. Use right away, or store in an airtight container in the refrigerator for up to 5 days or in zip-top plastic bags in the freezer for up to 2 months.

MAKES 4 QUARTS/4 LITERS

Easy Overnight Chicken Stock

If you want to make a smaller amount of stock, try Michael's recipe for overnight stock. It's something to make whenever you've roasted a chicken or even if you've brought home a rotisserie chicken from the grocery store. Simply break up the carcass, put it in a saucepan with carrot and onion (and any other aromatics you might have on hand), cover it all with water, and put it in a low oven overnight, then strain. Can't be beat for deliciousness or utility.

- 1 roast chicken carcass
- 1 onion, quartered
- 1 or 2 carrots
- ½ teaspoon salt
  Optional, any or all of the following: 1 bay leaf, flat-leaf parsley sprigs, 1 tablespoon tomato paste, 1 teaspoon whole black peppercorns
  About 2 quarts/2 liters water

1. Combine the chicken carcass, onion, carrots, salt, and optional add-ins in a medium oven-safe saucepan. Pour in enough water to cover the ingredients by 2 to 3 inches/5 to 7.5 centimeters. Put the pan, uncovered, in the oven and turn the oven to 200°F/95°C.

2. In the morning, or after 8 hours, strain the stock through a fine-mesh sieve into a clean container or pan. Use right away, or store in an airtight container in the refrigerator for up to 5 days or in a zip-top plastic bag in the freezer for up to 2 months.

MAKES 1 QUART/1 LITER

YELLOW MUSTARD

Mustard is the most versatile condiment when it comes to pies. And in our opinion, French's yellow mustard is the standard American mustard. It is, of course, the perfect hot dog condiment—indeed, it was introduced on a hot dog, at the 1904 World Fair in St. Louis, by Robert and George French. But it's great for almost any pie, especially any made with pork.

Yellow mustards are not difficult to make. Here we offer three simple mustard recipes to try. All of them begin with dry mustard (our go-to is Colman's mustard powder). The first is simply equal parts dry mustard and water, which is the condiment you'd get at a Chinese restaurant. This one is hot, but you can add brown sugar to offset the heat.

The second is also hot; it builds on the first with the addition of vinegar, brown sugar, and egg. This is a cooked preparation.

And finally the faux French's, which uses Wondra flour for the consistency. Wondra is a cooked and dehydrated flour that is very fine and dissolves in liquid quickly without clumping. The mustard will be slightly grainy, as the smoothness of commercial products requires industrial machinery.

Hot Mustard #1

This is a very loose mustard in the style of Chinese mustard, hot and delicious.

- 6 tablespoons/48 grams Colman's mustard powder
- 1 teaspoon brown sugar (optional)
- 6 tablespoons/90 milliliters water

1. Combine all of the ingredients in a bowl and whisk until smooth. Let stand for 15 minutes before using. Store in an airtight container in the refrigerator for up to 1 month.

MAKES ½ CUP/120 MILLILITERS

Hot Mustard #2

This is what we call a pub mustard, one thickened with egg. It's creamier than Hot Mustard #1 (above) but still has some heat.

- 1 large egg
- 5 tablespoons/40 grams Colman's mustard powder
- 5 tablespoons/75 milliliters distilled white vinegar
- 2 tablespoons brown sugar

1. Combine all of the ingredients in a metal bowl and whisk together. Place the bowl over a pot of simmering water and whisk continuously until thickened, about 10 minutes. Remove from the heat and let cool before serving.

2. Store in an airtight container in the refrigerator for up to 1 month.

MAKES 1 CUP/240 MILLILITERS

Faux French's Yellow American Mustard

When Brian had restaurants in Detroit, he used to make everything in house. *Everything*—even ketchup. It's instructive to make condiments, ones that you would typically buy at the store. Such is the case with mustard. He loves French's yellow mustard, so he wanted to make his own version to see how it worked. This mustard is just like what you buy in the store, only a little more fun and a little bit better.

- ⅓ cup/80 milliliters water
- 5 tablespoons/40 grams Colman's mustard powder
- ¼ cup/60 milliliters distilled white vinegar
- 1 teaspoon Wondra flour or cornstarch
- ½ teaspoon ground turmeric
  Kosher salt and freshly ground black pepper to taste

1. Combine all of the ingredients in a small saucepan and mix well. Bring the mixture to a gentle simmer over medium heat and simmer for 5 minutes. Remove from the heat and allow to cool before using.

2. Store in an airtight container in the refrigerator for up to 1 month.

MAKES ¾ CUP/180 MILLILITERS

All-Purpose Gravy

Most pies, if they don't have their own sauce inside the crust, such as a pot pie, benefit greatly from a gravy.

The best gravy is made from the pan drippings after roasting a turkey or chicken, using that caramelized meat deliciousness stuck to the pan. Adding a little stock or water and wine to remove those flavorful nuggets and emulsifying the fat creates a solid pan jus or gravy. But we don't always have flavorful drippings to make use of. Fortunately, there are other ways to make a great all-purpose gravy that can be served with just about any meat pie.

You are essentially making a very rich flavorful stock and thickening it (see Thickening Strategies, page 46). For this gravy, we do add one additional thickener: Wondra flour. This is a low-protein cooked flour that is dried and finely ground. Sprinkle it into hot stock and there will be no lumps or raw flour flavor. Use 1 tablespoon to thicken 1 cup/240 milliliters stock. But because you're cooking it, all-purpose flour works as well.

    1 tablespoon vegetable oil
    ½ onion, thinly sliced
    1 pound/450 grams chicken leg/thigh meat, neck
      bones, and/or gizzards, skin and fat removed
    1 quart/1 liter unsalted chicken stock or water
    8 thyme sprigs
      Small bunch fresh flat-leaf parsley
    1 bay leaf
    8 whole black peppercorns, cracked with the flat
      side of a knife or a sauté pan
  1½ ounces/45 grams unsalted butter
    6 tablespoons/45 grams Wondra flour
      Juice of ¼ lemon
      Kosher salt and freshly ground black pepper
      to taste

1. Heat the oil in a large saucepan over medium-high heat. Add the onion, meat, and bones and cook, stirring often, to brown the meat and bones, 8 to 10 minutes.

2. Add the stock, thyme, parsley, bay leaf, and peppercorns and bring to a boil. Turn the heat down to the gentlest possible simmer and simmer for 2 hours. Strain through a fine-mesh sieve.

3. Melt the butter in a small, thick-bottomed saucepan over medium-low heat. Whisk in the flour to make a paste and cook for 5 to 6 minutes, stirring frequently with a flat-edged wooden spoon.

4. Slowly pour in the hot stock, while whisking continuously, then simmer for 20 minutes.

5. Use right away, or store in an airtight container in the refrigerator for up to 5 days or in the freezer for up to 1 month.

MAKES 2 CUPS/480 MILLILITERS

Note: You can change the flavor of your gravy to fit your pie. Of course, you don't have to start with chicken. You can make a beef, pork, or lamb gravy in exactly the same way. Make sure the bones you have include joints, which contain abundant gelatin that gives the stock more body.

In addition to changing the protein, there are other ways to finesse a gravy at the end of cooking it:

- To make a lighter, slightly acidic, gravy, reduce 1 cup/240 milliliters dry white wine to ¼ cup/60 milliliters and add it to the gravy.
- For a more complex and elegant gravy, add ¼ cup/60 milliliters Cognac, dry sherry, or bourbon.
- For a creamy gravy, you guessed it—add heavy cream, about ½ cup/120 milliliters.
- For a rich and velvety gravy, whip in 4 ounces/115 grams soft unsalted butter and ¼ cup/60 milliliters heavy cream.
- To enhance the gravy and give it an umami blast, sauté 8 ounces/225 grams sliced mushrooms with 1 tablespoon minced shallot and add this to the gravy.
- If you like a smoky gravy, cut 5 strips of bacon into thin strips, sauté them until crisp, drain the fat, and add the bacon to the gravy.

Red Currant Sauce

Red currant sauce, a combination of red currant jelly, port, citrus zest, and mustard, can be served warm or room temperature. It goes especially well with duck, like the American Pekin Duck Pie with Pistachios (page 134). Serving a sweet-spicy sauce balances the strong flavor of the meat and offsets its richness.

1½ cups/360 milliliters red currant jelly
1 cup/240 milliliters ruby red port wine
3 tablespoons minced shallot
Grated zest and juice of 1 orange
Grated zest and juice of 1 lemon
2 teaspoons Colman's mustard powder
1 teaspoon kosher salt

1. Combine all of the ingredients in a small, heavy-bottomed saucepan and bring to a simmer over medium heat. Cook until slightly thick, 12 to 15 minutes, stirring to remove any lumps.

2. Strain through a fine-mesh sieve. Use immediately, or store in an airtight container in the refrigerator for up to 2 weeks. Reheat it or allow it to come to room temperature before serving.

MAKES 2 CUPS/480 MILLILITERS

Mustard-Horseradish-Dill Sauce

This cold, mayonnaise-based sauce goes well with any meat pie, but especially pork, chicken, and fish. Fresh horseradish root can be used, but a good store-bought prepared horseradish works just as well. Be sure to drain the prepared horseradish well. It's critical to use fresh dill, which really makes the sauce. This sauce comes together in 5 minutes.

¾ cup/180 milliliters mayonnaise
¼ cup/60 milliliters sour cream
3 tablespoons Dijon mustard
2 tablespoons prepared horseradish, well drained
2 teaspoons freshly squeezed lemon juice
2 tablespoons chopped fresh dill
  Kosher salt and freshly ground black pepper to taste

1. Combine all of the ingredients in a bowl and mix well. Use right away, or store in an airtight container in the refrigerator for up to 1 week.

MAKES ABOUT 1½ CUPS/360 MILLILITERS

Apple Horseradish

This is a combination of two simple ingredients—fresh horseradish root and apple—with some acid, lemon juice. Serve this condiment at room temperature or cold. It's especially fine with braised red meats, such as the Beef Short Rib and Vegetable Pot Pie with Red Wine Sauce (page 51).

2 Granny Smith apples
  Juice of 1 lemon
  Kosher salt and freshly ground black pepper to taste
1 (1-inch/2.5-centimeter) piece horseradish root, peeled

1. Grate the unpeeled apples on the shredder side of a box grater into a bowl, stopping when you get to the core. Add the lemon juice and season with salt and pepper.

2. Grate the horseradish root to the same size, being careful not the scrape your knuckles—hold on to the root with a towel so it has less chance of slipping. Toss all the ingredients together.

3. Use right away, or store in an airtight container in the refrigerator for up to 1 week. Squeeze out any excess juice before serving.

MAKES ABOUT 1 CUP/240 MILLILITERS

Apple Horseradish Mayonnaise

In this condiment, the apples are cooked and pureed rather than used raw as in the Apple Horseradish (left), and mayonnaise adds a richness and smoothness. It's best to use a tart baking apple, such as Granny Smith. If you only have access to a sweeter apple, increase the lemon juice, as the acidity is important in this condiment. This sauce pairs perfectly with pork and game.

2 Granny Smith apples, peeled, cored, and sliced
Juice of 1 lemon
1 tablespoon dry white wine
2 cups/480 milliliters mayonnaise
2 tablespoons prepared horseradish root, well drained
Kosher salt and freshly ground black pepper to taste

1. Combine the apples, lemon juice, and wine in a medium saucepan, cover, and cook over medium heat until tender, 10 or 15 minutes.

2. Transfer the mixture to a food processor and puree until smooth. Return the pureed mixture to the saucepan and cook over medium heat, stirring continuously, until the mixture is stiff and dry, allowing all the water to evaporate, 5 to 6 minutes. Allow to cool, then refrigerate until chilled.

3. Combine the chilled apple puree, mayonnaise, and horseradish in a bowl. Season with salt and pepper and add more lemon juice if needed. Use right away, or store in an airtight container in the refrigerator for up to 1 week.

MAKES ABOUT 3 CUPS/720 MILLILITERS

Sweet Onion Sauce

This warm sauce is a take on the classic soubise sauce, a béchamel (roux-thickened milk) flavored with abundant cooked onions. In classical cuisine it is often thickened with rice, but cream is richer and there are enough onions to serve as the thickening agent. It's important to cook the onions well without browning them so that this is a snow-white sauce. This sauce goes especially well with pork and chicken dishes.

2 ounces/60 grams unsalted butter
1 pound/450 grams sweet onions, thinly sliced
1 cup/240 milliliters heavy cream
Kosher salt and freshly ground black pepper to taste

1. In a large, heavy-bottomed skillet, melt the butter over medium heat. Add the onions, cover, and turn the heat down to medium-low. Cook the onions until they are soft and all their juices have been released but they are not browned, 12 to 15 minutes.

2. Add the cream, bring to a simmer, and reduce until the cream will coat the back of a spoon, 8 to 10 minutes. Taste and season with salt and pepper.

3. Transfer the mixture to a blender and puree until smooth. If you wish, pass the mixture through a fine-mesh sieve for a delectable texture. Use right away, or store an airtight container in the refrigerator for up to 5 days.

MAKES ABOUT 2 CUPS/480 MILLILITERS

Mushroom Jus Lié

This very simple all-purpose sauce works with any meat pie in the book. It couldn't be more straightforward: Mushrooms are seared for flavor, then cooked with shallot, sherry, and stock. It's thickened with a cornstarch slurry, just like a traditional meat jus. To make a vegetarian sauce, use vegetable stock.

- 3 tablespoons vegetable oil
- 1 pound/450 grams button mushrooms, sliced ¼ inch/6 millimeters thick
- 2 tablespoons minced shallot
- ½ cup/120 milliliters dry sherry
- 2 cups/480 milliliters chicken or beef stock
- 2 tablespoons cornstarch slurry (see page 46), or as needed
  Kosher salt and freshly ground black pepper to taste

1. Heat the oil in a large, heavy-bottomed skillet over medium-high heat. When the oil is almost smoking, add the mushrooms and brown, 10 to 12 minutes. Add the shallot, then deglaze with the sherry and cook until dry, 5 to 6 minutes.

2. Add the stock and bring to a boil. Thicken with the cornstarch slurry until it coats the back of a spoon (this is known as nappé consistency). Season with salt and pepper. If you wish, blend the sauce and pass it through a fine-mesh sieve for an elegant texture.

MAKES ABOUT 2 CUPS/480 MILLILITERS

Apricot and Sweet Onion Chutney

This condiment goes well with all meat pies, especially the Duck Confit Pie (page 146). The sweetness from the apricots and honey is balanced by the tartness from the lemon juice and vinegar. Make this one ahead of time and store in a container with a tight-fitting lid for up to a month in the refrigerator.

- 1 tablespoon/15 milliliters vegetable oil
- 4 ounces/115 grams sweet onion, thinly sliced and cut into 1-inch/2.5-centimeter lengths
- 4 ounces/115 grams dried apricots, small dice
- 1 tablespoon/15 milliliters fresh lemon juice
- 1 teaspoon/3 grams lemon zest
- 2 ounces/60 grams honey
- 1 tablespoon/15 milliliters soy sauce
- 4 ounces/115 milliliters lager beer
- 1 tablespoon/15 milliliters white wine vinegar
- 1 ounce/30 grams toasted sliced almonds

1. Heat the oil in a heavy-bottomed saucepan over medium heat. When the oil is hot, add the onion and sauté until soft but not browned, about 5 minutes. Add the remaining ingredients except for the almonds, raise the heat to medium high, and bring it all to a simmer, then reduce the heat to low and cook for 15 to 20 minutes or until lightly thick. Set aside to cool.

2. Fold in the almonds and store the chutney in an airtight container in the refrigerator for up to a month.

MAKES ABOUT 1½ CUPS/350 MILLILITERS

Red Onion Relish

Brian loves pickled vegetables with pies, especially pickled red onions. This condiment is sweet and almost jam-like. Onion and garlic, honey, red wine, and red wine vinegar—that's it. Red onion relish is great on smoked meat, sandwiches, and both meat and vegetable pies, such as Mediterranean Vegetable Pie (page 88) or Pork and Duck Confit Pie (page 139).

  1 tablespoon/15 milliliters vegetable oil
  1 pound/450 grams thinly sliced red onion
  2 tablespoons/30 milliliters minced garlic
  4 ounces/115 grams honey
  3 ounces/90 milliliters dry red wine
  2 ounces/60 milliliters red wine vinegar
    Kosher salt and freshly ground black pepper
    to taste

1. Heat the oil in a thick-bottomed sauté pan over medium heat. When the oil is hot, add the onion and garlic. Lower the heat to low and cook until the onion is golden brown and lightly caramelized, 5 to 8 minutes.

2. Turn the heat to high and add the honey, red wine, and vinegar. When it comes to a simmer, lower the heat to medium and cook 5 to 8 minutes or until it is a syrupy consistency. Season with salt and pepper.

3. Cool and store in an airtight container in the refrigerator for up to a week.

MAKES ABOUT 2 CUPS/480 MILLILITERS

Roasted Red Pepper Relish

Red peppers have a natural sweetness, and roasting them not only facilitates removing the skin but also adds a pleasing charred flavor. This relish pairs best with fish or vegetable pies such as the Tomato, Basil, and Mozzarella Pie (page 130) or the Salmon Rolled Pie (page 96). Choose a good aged balsamic to compliment the sweetness and introduce a little acid.

  2 red peppers
  2 ounces/60 milliliters olive oil
  4 ounces/115 grams thinly sliced sweet onion
  1 ounce /30 grams pitted kalamata olives,
    coarsely chopped
  1 tablespoon/15 milliliters chopped fresh basil
  1 ounce/30 milliliters aged balsamic vinegar
    Kosher salt and freshly ground black pepper
    to taste

1. Over an open flame of a gas burner char the peppers black, allowing the skin to blister. Place in a bowl and cover with plastic wrap until cool enough to handle. (Alternately, halve the peppers and broil until charred, then place in a bowl and cover.)

2. Heat the oil in a thick-bottomed skillet over medium heat. When the oil is hot, sauté the onions until soft but without color, about 5 minutes.

3. Peel and seed the peppers after they've cooled. Cut them into a ¼-inch/6-millimeter dice. Add the peppers to the onion along with the olives, basil, and balsamic vinegar. Season with salt and pepper. Store the relish in an airtight container in the refrigerator for up to a week.

MAKES ABOUT 2 CUPS/480 MILLILITERS

Summer Tomato Tart (page 120)

Acknowledgments

From Brian:

I've been teaching charcuterie and butchery at the college level since 1997. During that time I have watched how the student body has changed, from entire classes made up of kids right out of high school to people who have retired from their profession and just want to learn to cook. As I prepare for my retirement this year, I have to say that my current group of students may be the best I've ever had. Maybe it's because I know they will be my last and I will be free! It took longer to write this book than any of the other three Michael and I have written. This book has been in the works for four years. (COVID didn't help.) Over that time nearly everyone in my classes (mostly unknowingly) contributed something to this book testing recipes. The most recent group not only did that but also helped organize, prep, and execute the food for the sixty-plus photos that appear in this book. Photography was shot over a three-day period and almost killed me. Thank you Quentin Bacon for your outstanding images.

I'd like to thank my son Dylan (number four of five), who lent his skills as a hand model for all the process shots after Ruhlman ruled my fat, hairy fingers out; Vera Lone, my sous chef, who at eighteen has accomplished more than most forty-year-olds; Adam Wolf (who's always sorry); Mia Johnson; Allison White; Kara O'Sullivan (another good sous chef); Tyler Johnson; Maddie Grupa; Jordon Demchak; Janine Esshaki (fish pie woman); and Mitayel Payne (snoop dog). All of you did a great job and gained invaluable culinary knowledge doing this most important project.

As I've always said, it's a pleasure teaching at Schoolcraft College. The administration truly supports the culinary program. I'd like to thank my colleagues Brian Beland CMC, Drew Sayes CMC, Marcus Haight, Paul Grocz BMF, Jeff Gabriel CMC, and Heather Moore CMB for all the support you've given me personally and the contributions you've made to this book.

Lastly I'd like to thank my buddy and coauthor, Michael Ruhlman, for being so talented, calling me out when necessary, and being my confidant and friend these past twenty-some years. Cheers, pal.

—

From Michael:

And to you, brother. I couldn't be more grateful for you, the collaboration, or your friendship.

I know you join me in thanking the editor of this book, Melanie Tortoroli, for giving us the opportunity to explore the world of savory pies. Her assistant, Annabel Brazaitis, did the daily grind work—without which all the other work would have fallen apart. Our longtime copyeditor, Karen Wise, did her usual extraordinary work on this book to make sure not only that the prose was clean but also that all the recipes made sense and were consistent, and she also kept us from getting too "cheffy" on the reader. It's a huge job and we're grateful.

There are many people who help to birth a book, some of whom we never meet. But they, too, are invaluable. The art director for this book was Allison Chi. Susan Sanfrey was the project editor. The project manager was Anna Oler. Meredith McGinnis is the book's marketer. The excellent Will Scarlett is its publicist. Lynne Cannon Menges proofread the finished, copyedited pages, and Elizabeth Parson created the index.

We'd also like to thank Calum Franklin, Great Britain's pie virtuoso, for always being available to discuss pies.

Thank you again to our photographer, Quentin Bacon, who made the food look better in pictures than it did coming out of the oven.

Pork Tenderloin with Root Vegetables and
Mushrooms in Puff Pastry (page 98)

2-1

tart shells

Index

Note: Page references in *italics* indicate recipe photographs.

A

Ale, Beef, and Onion Hand-Raised Pies, *74*, 75–76
American Pekin Duck Pie with Pistachios, 134–37, *137*
apples
    Apple, Cabbage, and Blue Cheese Slaw, 183
    Apple Horseradish, 194
    Apple Horseradish Mayonnaise, 195
    Curried Duck or Chicken Turnovers, 158
Apricot and Sweet Onion Chutney, 196
Arugula or Watercress, Roasted Beets with, 185
Asparagus and Creamed Morel Vol-au-Vents, 173
Atlantic Salmon in Puff Pastry, 144–45

B

bacon
    Chicken, Mushroom, and Bacon Sheet Pan Pie, *142*, 143
    Chicken and Ham Hand-Raised Pies, 80–81
    Chicken Sheet Pan Pie, *8*, 140–41
bacon, Canadian
    Country Sausage Roll, 99
    Hand-Raised Pork Pies, *66*, 70–71
Baked Puff Pastry Rounds, 54, *55*
basil
    Mediterranean Vegetable Pie, 88–90, *91*
    Summer Tomato Tart, 120, *121*
    Tomato, Basil, and Mozzarella Pie, 130, *131*
beef
    Beef, Onion, and Ale Hand-Raised Pies, *74*, 75–76
    Beef and Bone Marrow Pot Pie, 61–62, *63*
    Beef Short Rib and Vegetable Pot Pie with Red Wine Sauce, *50*, 51–52
    Cornish-Style Pasties, *152*, 156–57
    Individual Pot Roast Pies with Roasted Carrots and Caramelized Onions, *148*, 149–51
    Michigan Upper Peninsula Pasties, 155
Beets, Roasted, with Arugula or Watercress, 185

bench scraper, 22
beurre manié, about, 46
biscuit crust
    about, 29
    Biscuit Crust, *47*, 49
    Chicken Pot Pie with Biscuit Crust, *47*, 48–49
blind baking, 25
blitz puff pastry dough
    about, 29
    Baked Puff Pastry Rounds, 54, *55*
    Blitz Puff Pastry Dough, 36–40, *37–40*
    working with, rules for, 167
blitz puff pastry dough (recipes with)
    Atlantic Salmon in Puff Pastry, 144–45
    Beef Short Rib and Vegetable Pot Pie with Red Wine Sauce, *50*, 51–52
    Crawfish and Andouille Vol-au-Vents, *174*, 175
    Creamed Morel and Asparagus Vol-au-Vents, 173
    Emincé of Chicken with Lemon, Tarragon, and Garlic Vol-au-Vents, *171*, 177
    Escargots with Parsley and Garlic Vol-au-Vents, 170, *171*
    Guinea Fowl Pot Pie, *42*, 53–54, *55*
    Haddock, Corn, and Potato Pot Pie, *58*, 59
    Lamb Loin en Croûte with Spinach and Pine Nuts, 85–87, *87*
    Mediterranean Vegetable Pie, 88–90, *91*
    Pork Tenderloin with Root Vegetables and Mushrooms in Puff Pastry, 98, *201*
    Roasted Vegetable Pot Pie, 56
    Sautéed Gulf Shrimp with Cognac and Cream Vol-au-Vents, *171*, 172
    Seared Sea Scallop with Sweet Corn and Roasted Red Pepper Vol-au-Vents, 176
    Tomato, Basil, and Mozzarella Pie, 130, *131*
    Venison Pot Pie, 64, *65*
    Vol-au-Vent Pastry Shells, 168–69, *169*
    Wild Mushroom and Leek Pot Pie, 57

Bone Marrow and Beef Pot Pie, 61–62, *63*
bourbon
    Sweet Potato Galette, 122–23, *123*
box grater, 22
Brian's Mashed Potatoes, 181
butter, 24

C

cabbage
    Apple, Cabbage, and Blue Cheese Slaw, 183
    Quick-Pickled Red Cabbage, 184
Canadian bacon
    Country Sausage Roll, 99
    Hand-Raised Pork Pies, *66*, 70–71
carrots
    Beef Short Rib and Vegetable Pot Pie with Red Wine Sauce, *50*, 51–52
    Carrot and Parsnip Mash, *178*, 185
    Cornish-Style Pasties, *152*, 156–57
    Honey-Garlic Roasted Carrots, *178*, 182
    Individual Pot Roast Pies with Roasted Carrots and Caramelized Onions, *148*, 149–51
    Michigan Upper Peninsula Pasties, 155
    Pork Tenderloin with Root Vegetables and Mushrooms in Puff Pastry, 98, *201*
    Roasted Vegetable Pot Pie, 56
cashews
    Curried Duck or Chicken Turnovers, 158
cauliflower
    Roasted Curried Cauliflower Turnovers, 160, *161*
    Roasted Vegetable Pot Pie, 56
chalazae, 28
cheese
    Apple, Cabbage, and Blue Cheese Slaw, 183
    The Best Mushroom Tart, *124*, 125
    Five-Onion Pie, 106, *107*
    German Heirloom Cottage Cheese Pie, 105

cheese (*continued*)
    Leek and Potato Pie, *110*, 111
    Leek Gratin Pie, 109
    Mediterranean Vegetable Pie, 88–90, *91*
    Mom's Pierogis, 162, *163*
    Smoked Atlantic Haddock Pie, 112, *113*
    Spanish Chorizo, Goat Cheese, and
        Red Pepper Pie, *114*, 115
    Spinach and Mushroom Galette, 116,
        117
    Stilton Cheesecake with Walnut
        Crust, *118*, 119
    Summer Tomato Tart, 120, *121*
    Tomato, Basil, and Mozzarella Pie,
        130, *131*
Cheesecake, Stilton, with Walnut Crust,
    118, 119
chicken
    Chicken, Mushroom, and Bacon
        Sheet Pan Pie, *142*, 143
    Chicken, Pork, Liver, and Mushroom
        Hand-Raised Pies, 77–78, *79*
    Chicken and Ham Hand-Raised Pies,
        80–81
    Chicken Pot Pie with Biscuit Crust,
        47, 48–49
    Chicken Sheet Pan Pie, *8*, 140–41
    Chicken Stock, 189
    Curried Duck or Chicken Turnovers, 158
    Easy Overnight Chicken Stock, 189
    Emincé of Chicken with Lemon,
        Tarragon, and Garlic Vol-au-
        Vents, *171*, 177
Chickpea Turnovers, Curried, 159
Chutney, Apricot and Sweet Onion, 196
Cognac and Cream, Sautéed Gulf
    Shrimp with, Vol-au-Vents, *171*, 172
corn
    Haddock, Corn, and Potato Pot Pie,
        58, 59
    Seared Sea Scallop with Sweet Corn
        and Roasted Red Pepper Vol-au-
        Vents, 176
Cornish-Style Pasties, *152*, 156–57
Cottage Cheese Pie, German Heirloom,
    105
Country Sausage Roll, 99
couscous
    Mediterranean Vegetable Pie, 88–90, *91*
Crawfish and Andouille Vol-au-Vents,
    174, 175
crêpes
    Crêpes, *26*, 27
    lining dough with, 27
crêpes (recipes with)
    Atlantic Salmon in Puff Pastry, 144–45
    Lamb Loin en Croûte with Spinach
        and Pine Nuts, 85–87, *87*
    Poached Salmon and Dill Rolled Pie,
        92, 93–95
    Pork Tenderloin with Root Vegetables
        and Mushrooms in Puff Pastry,
        98, *201*
Cucumber and Smoked Ham Salad,
    178, 183
Cumberland-Style Sausage Rolls, 100,
    101

Curried Cauliflower, Roasted,
    Turnovers, 160, *161*
Curried Chickpea Turnovers, 159
Curried Duck or Chicken Turnovers, 158

D

Diamond Crystal salt, 19
digital scale, 20
digital thermometer, 22
dill
    Hot-Smoked Salmon and Dill Pie, 108
    Mustard-Horseradish-Dill Sauce, *186*,
        194
    Poached Salmon and Dill Rolled Pie,
        92, 93–95
docker, 20–22
dolly, pie, 20
double-crusted pies
    about, 128
    American Pekin Duck Pie with
        Pistachios, 134–37, *137*
    Atlantic Salmon in Puff Pastry,
        144–45
    Braised Pork and Lentil Pie, 138
    Chicken, Mushroom, and Bacon
        Sheet Pan Pie, *142*, 143
    Chicken Sheet Pan Pie, *8*, 140–41
    Individual Duck Confit Pies, 146, *147*
    Individual Pot Roast Pies
        with Roasted Carrots and
        Caramelized Onions, *148*, 149–51
    Pork and Duck Confit Pie, 139
    Post-Thanksgiving Turkey Pot Pie, *132*,
        133
    Tomato, Basil, and Mozzarella Pie,
        130, *131*
dough basics, 24–41
    blind baking, 25
    crimping process, 30–31
    decorating dough, 28
    egg wash, 28
    filling basics, 27
    flour, fat, and water, 24
    miscellaneous doughs, 29
    moisture barriers, 25–27
    note about dough yields, 29
    rolling out, 24–25
    three primary doughs, 28–29
    vent hole, 27
dough crimper, 22
dough cutter, 22
dough recipes
    Biscuit Crust, *47*, 49
    Blitz Puff Pastry Dough, 36–40,
        37–40
    Gluten-Free Dough, 41
    Hot-Water Dough, 70, *72–73*
    Pâte Brisée, 33, *34*
    Sour Cream Pastry Dough, 105
    3-2-1 Pie Dough, 33, *34–35*, 129
duck
    American Pekin Duck Pie with
        Pistachios, 134–37, *137*
    Curried Duck or Chicken Turnovers, 158
    Individual Duck Confit Pies, 146, *147*
    Pork and Duck Confit Pie, 139

E

eggplant
    Mediterranean Vegetable Pie, 88–90,
        91
eggs
    Atlantic Salmon in Puff Pastry,
        144–45
    Egg Wash, 28
    egg wash, purpose of, 28
    Poached Salmon and Dill Rolled Pie,
        92, 93–95
Escargots with Parsley and Garlic Vol-
    au-Vents, 170, *171*

F

fats, 24
Faux French's Yellow American
    Mustard, *186*, 191
Fennel, Shaved, and Red Onion Salad,
    184
fine-mesh sieve, 23
fish
    Atlantic Salmon in Puff Pastry,
        144–45
    Fish Pot Pie, 60
    Haddock, Corn, and Potato Pot Pie,
        58, 59
    Hot-Smoked Salmon and Dill Pie, 108
    Poached Salmon and Dill Rolled Pie,
        92, 93–95
    Salmon Rolled Pie with Shrimp and
        Spinach Mousseline, 96, *97*
    Smoked Atlantic Haddock Pie, 112,
        113
Five-Onion Pie, 106, *107*
flour
    flour-and-fat thickener, 46
    gluten-free, buying, 41
    role in doughs, 24

G

galettes
    about, 104
    Spinach and Mushroom Galette, 116,
        117
    Sweet Potato Galette, 122–23, *123*
garlic
    Chicken Sheet Pan Pie, *8*, 140–41
    Country Sausage Roll, 99
    Emincé of Chicken with Lemon,
        Tarragon, and Garlic Vol-au-
        Vents, *171*, 177
    Escargots with Parsley and Garlic
        Vol-au-Vents, 170, *171*
    Hand-Raised Pork Pies, *66*, 70–71
    Honey-Garlic Roasted Carrots, *178*,
        182
    how to roast, 71
    Potato and Garlic Puree, 182
German Heirloom Cottage Cheese Pie,
    105
gluten-free
    Gluten-Free Dough, 41
    gluten-free dough, substituting, 29
    gluten-free flours, buying, 41

gravy
    All-Purpose Gravy, 192
    changing flavor of, 193
    ways to finesse, 193
green beans
    Fish Pot Pie, 60
grinder, 22
Guinea Fowl Pot Pie, *42*, 53–54, *55*

H

haddock
    Haddock, Corn, and Potato Pot Pie,
        58, 59
    Smoked Atlantic Haddock Pie, 112,
        113
ham
    American Pekin Duck Pie with
        Pistachios, 134–37, *137*
    Chicken and Ham Hand-Raised Pies,
        80–81
    Country Sausage Roll, 99
    Cucumber and Smoked Ham Salad,
        178, 183
    Hand-Raised Pork Pies, *66*, 70–71
hand-raised pies
    about, 68
    Beef, Onion, and Ale Hand-Raised
        Pies, *74*, 75–76
    Chicken, Pork, Liver, and Mushroom
        Hand-Raised Pies, 77–78, *79*
    Chicken and Ham Hand-Raised Pies,
        80–81
    Hand-Raised Pork Pies, *66*, 70–71
herbs. *See* basil; dill; parsley
Honey-Garlic Roasted Carrots, *178*, 182
horseradish
    Apple Horseradish, 194
    Apple Horseradish Mayonnaise, 195
    Mustard-Horseradish-Dill Sauce, *186*,
        194
Hot Mustard #1, *186*, 191
Hot Mustard #2, *186*, 191
Hot-Smoked Salmon and Dill Pie, 108
hot-water dough
    about, 29
    Hot-Water Dough, 70, *72–73*
hot-water dough (recipes with)
    Beef, Onion, and Ale Hand-Raised
        Pies, *74*, 75–76
    Chicken, Pork, Liver, and Mushroom
        Hand-Raised Pies, 77–78, *79*
    Chicken and Ham Hand-Raised Pies,
        80–81
    Hand-Raised Pork Pies, *66*, 70–71

K

knives, 23
kosher salt, 19

L

Lamb Loin en Croûte with Spinach and
    Pine Nuts, 85–87, *87*
lard, 24
lattice cutter, 20

leeks
    Five-Onion Pie, 106, *107*
    Leek and Potato Pie, *110*, 111
    Leek Gratin Pie, 109
    Smoked Atlantic Haddock Pie, 112,
        113
    Wild Mushroom and Leek Pot Pie, 57
Lemon, Tarragon, and Garlic, Emincé of
    Chicken with, Vol-au-Vents, *171*, 177
Lentil and Braised Pork Pie, 138
Liver, Chicken, Pork, and Mushroom
    Hand-Raised Pies, 77–78, *79*

M

Madeira wine
    American Pekin Duck Pie with
        Pistachios, 134–37, *137*
    Spinach and Mushroom Galette, 116,
        117
mayonnaise-based sauces
    Apple Horseradish Mayonnaise, 195
    Mustard-Horseradish-Dill Sauce, *186*,
        194
meat. *See* beef; lamb; pork; venison
meat grinder, 22
meat pies, history of, 11–14
Mediterranean Vegetable Pie, 88–90,
    91
Michigan Upper Peninsula Pasties, 155
mixer, standing, 22
Mom's Pierogis, 162, *163*
Morton's kosher salt, 19
mushrooms
    Atlantic Salmon in Puff Pastry,
        144–45
    The Best Mushroom Tart, *124*, 125
    Chicken, Mushroom, and Bacon
        Sheet Pan Pie, *142*, 143
    Chicken, Pork, Liver, and Mushroom
        Hand-Raised Pies, 77–78, *79*
    Chicken Pot Pie with Biscuit Crust,
        47, 48–49
    Country Sausage Roll, 99
    Creamed Morel and Asparagus Vol-
        au-Vents, 173
    Guinea Fowl Pot Pie, *42*, 53–54, 55
    Haddock, Corn, and Potato Pot Pie,
        58, 59
    Mushroom Jus Lié, 196
    Poached Salmon and Dill Rolled Pie,
        92, 93–95
    Pork and Duck Confit Pie, 139
    Pork Tenderloin with Root Vegetables
        and Mushrooms in Puff Pastry,
        98, *201*
    Roasted Vegetable Pot Pie, 56
    Smoked Atlantic Haddock Pie, 112,
        113
    Spinach and Mushroom Galette, 116,
        117
    Wild Mushroom and Leek Pot Pie, 57
mustard, 190
    Faux French's Yellow American
        Mustard, *186*, 191
    Hot Mustard #1, *186*, 191
    Hot Mustard #2, *186*, 191

    Mustard-Horseradish-Dill Sauce, *186*,
        194

O

offset spatula, 22
onions
    Apricot and Sweet Onion Chutney,
        196
    Beef, Onion, and Ale Hand-Raised
        Pies, *74*, 75–76
    Five-Onion Pie, 106, *107*
    Guinea Fowl Pot Pie, *42*, 53–54, *55*
    Hot-Smoked Salmon and Dill Pie, 108
    Individual Pot Roast Pies
        with Roasted Carrots and
        Caramelized Onions, *148*, 149–51
    Red Onion Relish, 197
    Roasted Vegetable Pot Pie, 56
    Shaved Fennel and Red Onion Salad,
        184
    Sweet Onion Sauce, 195
    Tomato, Basil, and Mozzarella Pie, 130,
        131

P

pans, 20
parchment paper, 22
Parsley and Garlic, Escargots with, Vol-
    au-Vents, 170, *171*
parsnips
    Carrot and Parsnip Mash, *178*, 185
    Pork Tenderloin with Root Vegetables
        and Mushrooms in Puff Pastry,
        98, *201*
pasties
    Cornish-Style Pasties, *152*, 156–57
    Michigan Upper Peninsula Pasties,
        155
pastry blender, 22
pastry brushes, 20
pâte brisée
    about, 29
    Pâte Brisée, 33, *34*
pâte brisée (recipes with)
    Beef and Bone Marrow Pot Pie,
        61–62, *63*
    The Best Mushroom Tart, *124*, 125
    Chicken, Mushroom, and Bacon
        Sheet Pan Pie, *142*, 143
    Country Sausage Roll, 99
    Cumberland-Style Sausage Rolls,
        100, *101*
    Curried Chickpea Turnovers, 159
    Five-Onion Pie, 106, *107*
    Hot-Smoked Salmon and Dill Pie, 108
    Individual Duck Confit Pies, 146, *147*
    Leek Gratin Pie, 109
    Poached Salmon and Dill Rolled Pie,
        92, 93–95
    Smoked Atlantic Haddock Pie, 112, *113*
    Spanish Chorizo, Goat Cheese, and
        Red Pepper Pie, *114*, 115
    Spinach and Mushroom Galette, 116,
        117
    Sweet Potato Galette, 122–23, *123*

peas
    Chicken Pot Pie with Biscuit Crust,
        47, 48–49
    Post-Thanksgiving Turkey Pot Pie,
        132, 133
peppers
    Mediterranean Vegetable Pie, 88–90, *91*
    Roasted Red Pepper Relish, 197
    Seared Sea Scallop with Sweet Corn
        and Roasted Red Pepper Vol-au-
        Vents, 176
    Spanish Chorizo, Goat Cheese, and
        Red Pepper Pie, *114*, 115
pie docker, 20–22
pie dolly, 20
Pierogis, Mom's, 162, *163*
pie weights, 22
Pine Nuts and Spinach, Lamb Loin en
    Croûte with, 85–87, *87*
Pistachios, American Pekin Duck Pie
    with, 134–37, *137*
pork. *See also* bacon; Canadian bacon;
    ham
    Braised Pork and Lentil Pie, 138
    Chicken, Mushroom, and Bacon
        Sheet Pan Pie, *142*, 143
    Chicken, Pork, Liver, and Mushroom
        Hand-Raised Pies, 77–78, *79*
    Country Sausage Roll, 99
    Crawfish and Andouille Vol-au-Vents,
        174, 175
    Cumberland-Style Sausage Rolls,
        100, *101*
    Hand-Raised Pork Pies, *66*, 70–71
    Lamb Loin en Croûte with Spinach
        and Pine Nuts, 85–87, *87*
    Michigan Upper Peninsula Pasties,
        155
    Pork and Duck Confit Pie, 139
    Pork Tenderloin with Root Vegetables
        and Mushrooms in Puff Pastry,
        98, *201*
    Spanish Chorizo, Goat Cheese, and
        Red Pepper Pie, *114*, 115
Post-Thanksgiving Turkey Pot Pie, *132*, 133
potatoes
    Beef and Bone Marrow Pot Pie, 61–62, *63*
    Beef Short Rib and Vegetable Pot Pie
        with Red Wine Sauce, *50*, 51–52
    Brian's Mashed Potatoes, 181
    Cornish-Style Pasties, *152*, 156–57
    Fish Pot Pie, 60
    Haddock, Corn, and Potato Pot Pie,
        58, 59
    Individual Pot Roast Pies
        with Roasted Carrots and
        Caramelized Onions, *148*, 149–51
    Leek and Potato Pie, *110*, 111
    Michigan Upper Peninsula Pasties, 155
    Pork and Duck Confit Pie, 139
    Potato and Garlic Puree, 182
    Roasted New Potato and Scallion
        Salad, *178*, 181
    Roasted Vegetable Pot Pie, 56
    Smoked Atlantic Haddock Pie, 112, *113*
    Sweet Potato Galette, 122–23, *123*
    Venison Pot Pie, 64, *65*
pot pie dishes, 20

pot pies
    about, 45
    Beef and Bone Marrow Pot Pie, 61–62, *63*
    Beef Short Rib and Vegetable Pot Pie
        with Red Wine Sauce, *50*, 51–52
    Chicken Pot Pie with Biscuit Crust,
        47, 48–49
    Fish Pot Pie, 60
    Guinea Fowl Pot Pie, *42*, 53–54, *55*
    Haddock, Corn, and Potato Pot Pie,
        58, 59
    Post-Thanksgiving Turkey Pot Pie, *132*,
        133
    Roasted Vegetable Pot Pie, 56
    thickening stock for, 46
    Venison Pot Pie, 64, *65*
    Wild Mushroom and Leek Pot Pie, 57
puff pastry. *See also* blitz puff pastry dough
    about, 28, 29
    working with, rules for, 167
Puree, Potato and Garlic, 182

Q

Quick-Pickled Red Cabbage, 184

R

Red Currant Sauce, 193
relish
    Red Onion Relish, 197
    Roasted Red Pepper Relish, 197
rice
    Atlantic Salmon in Puff Pastry, 144–45
rimmed baking sheets/sheet pans, 20
rolled raised pies
    about, 84
    Country Sausage Roll, 99
    Cumberland-Style Sausage Rolls,
        100, *101*
    Lamb Loin en Croûte with Spinach
        and Pine Nuts, 85–87, *87*
    Mediterranean Vegetable Pie, 88–90,
        91
    Poached Salmon and Dill Rolled Pie,
        92, 93–95
    Pork Tenderloin with Root Vegetables
        and Mushrooms in Puff Pastry,
        98, *201*
    Salmon Rolled Pie with Shrimp and
        Spinach Mousseline, 96, *97*
rolling pin, 20
round cutters, 22
roux, about, 46
ruler, 22
rutabaga
    Cornish-Style Pasties, *152*, 156–57
    Michigan Upper Peninsula Pasties, 155

S

salads
    Apple, Cabbage, and Blue Cheese
        Slaw, 183
    Cucumber and Smoked Ham Salad,
        178, 183
    Roasted New Potato and Scallion
        Salad, *178*, 181

Shaved Fennel and Red Onion Salad,
        184
salmon
    Atlantic Salmon in Puff Pastry,
        144–45
    Hot-Smoked Salmon and Dill Pie, 108
    Poached Salmon and Dill Rolled Pie,
        92, 93–95
    Salmon Rolled Pie with Shrimp and
        Spinach Mousseline, 96, *97*
salt, notes about, 19
sauces and condiments
    All-Purpose Gravy, 192
    Apple Horseradish, 194
    Apple Horseradish Mayonnaise, 195
    Apricot and Sweet Onion Chutney, 196
    Chicken Stock, 189
    Easy Overnight Chicken Stock, 189
    Faux French's Yellow American
        Mustard, *186*, 191
    Hot Mustard #1, *186*, 191
    Hot Mustard #2, *186*, 191
    Mushroom Jus Lié, 196
    Mustard-Horseradish-Dill Sauce,
        186, 194
    Red Currant Sauce, 193
    Red Onion Relish, 197
    Roasted Red Pepper Relish, 197
    Sweet Onion Sauce, 195
    yellow mustard, about, 190
sausages
    Country Sausage Roll, 99
    Crawfish and Andouille Vol-au-Vents,
        174, 175
    Cumberland-Style Sausage Rolls,
        100, *101*
    Spanish Chorizo, Goat Cheese, and
        Red Pepper Pie, *114*, 115
scale, digital, 20
scallions
    Five-Onion Pie, 106, *107*
    Hot-Smoked Salmon and Dill Pie, 108
    Roasted New Potato and Scallion
        Salad, *178*, 181
scissors, 22
Sea Scallop, Seared, with Sweet Corn
    and Roasted Red Pepper Vol-au-
    Vents, 176
sheet pan pies
    Chicken, Mushroom, and Bacon
        Sheet Pan Pie, *142*, 143
    Chicken Sheet Pan Pie, *8*, 140–41
shellfish
    Crawfish and Andouille Vol-au-Vents,
        174, 175
    Escargots with Parsley and Garlic
        Vol-au-Vents, 170, *171*
    Salmon Rolled Pie with Shrimp and
        Spinach Mousseline, 96, *97*
    Sautéed Gulf Shrimp with Cognac
        and Cream Vol-au-Vents, *171*, 172
    Seared Sea Scallop with Sweet Corn
        and Roasted Red Pepper Vol-au-
        Vents, 176
sherry
    The Best Mushroom Tart, *124*, 125
    Creamed Morel and Asparagus Vol-
        au-Vents, 173

Mushroom Jus Lié, 196
short dough, 24
shrimp
    Salmon Rolled Pie with Shrimp and
        Spinach Mousseline, 96, *97*
    Sautéed Gulf Shrimp with Cognac
        and Cream Vol-au-Vents, *171*, 172
sides
    Apple, Cabbage, and Blue Cheese
        Slaw, 183
    Brian's Mashed Potatoes, 181
    Carrot and Parsnip Mash, *178*, 185
    Cucumber and Smoked Ham Salad,
        178, 183
    Honey-Garlic Roasted Carrots, *178*, 182
    Potato and Garlic Puree, 182
    Quick-Pickled Red Cabbage, 184
    Roasted Beets with Arugula or
        Watercress, 185
    Roasted New Potato and Scallion
        Salad, *178*, 181
    Shaved Fennel and Red Onion Salad,
        184
sieve, fine-mesh, 23
single-crust pies
    about, 104
    The Best Mushroom Tart, *124*, 125
    Five-Onion Pie, 106, *107*
    German Heirloom Cottage Cheese
        Pie, 105
    Hot-Smoked Salmon and Dill Pie, 108
    Leek and Potato Pie, *110*, 111
    Leek Gratin Pie, 109
    Smoked Atlantic Haddock Pie, 112, *113*
    Spanish Chorizo, Goat Cheese, and
        Red Pepper Pie, *114*, 115
    Spinach and Mushroom Galette, 116,
        117
    Stilton Cheesecake with Walnut
        Crust, *118*, 119
    Summer Tomato Tart, 120, *121*
    Sweet Potato Galette, 122–23, *123*
Slaw, Apple, Cabbage, and Blue Cheese,
    183
slurry, about, 46
small offset spatula, 22
Smoked Atlantic Haddock Pie, 112, *113*
snails. *See* Escargots
sour cream pastry dough
    German Heirloom Cottage Cheese
        Pie, 105
    Sour Cream Pastry Dough, 105
Spanish Chorizo, Goat Cheese, and Red
    Pepper Pie, *114*, 115
spatula, small offset, 22
spinach
    Atlantic Salmon in Puff Pastry,
        144–45
    Individual Pot Roast Pies
        with Roasted Carrots and
        Caramelized Onions, *148*, 149–51
    Lamb Loin en Croûte with Spinach
        and Pine Nuts, 85–87, *87*
    Salmon Rolled Pie with Shrimp and
        Spinach Mousseline, 96, *97*
    Spinach and Mushroom Galette, 116,
        117

standing mixer, 22
stocks
    Chicken Stock, 189
    Easy Overnight Chicken Stock, 189
    thickening strategies, 46
    Turkey Stock, 133
Summer Tomato Tart, 120, *121*
Sweet Potato Galette, 122–23, *123*

T

Tarragon, Lemon, and Garlic, Emincé of
    Chicken with, Vol-au-Vents, *171*, 177
tarts
    about, 104
    The Best Mushroom Tart, *124*, 125
    Five-Onion Pie, 106, *107*
    German Heirloom Cottage Cheese
        Pie, 105
    Hot-Smoked Salmon and Dill Pie, 108
    Leek and Potato Pie, *110*, 111
    Leek Gratin Pie, 109
    Smoked Atlantic Haddock Pie, 112, *113*
    Spanish Chorizo, Goat Cheese, and
        Red Pepper Pie, *114*, 115
    Stilton Cheesecake with Walnut
        Crust, *118*, 119
    Summer Tomato Tart, 120, *121*
thermometer, 22
thickening stock, 46
3-2-1 dough
    about, 28
    3-2-1 Pie Dough, 33, *34–35*, 131
3-2-1 dough (recipes with)
    American Pekin Duck Pie with
        Pistachios, 134–37, *137*
    Braised Pork and Lentil Pie, 138
    Chicken Sheet Pan Pie, *8*, 140–41
    Cornish-Style Pasties, *152*, 156–57
    Curried Duck or Chicken Turnovers,
        158
    Individual Pot Roast Pies
        with Roasted Carrots and
        Caramelized Onions, *148*, 149–51
    Leek and Potato Pie, *110*, 111
    Michigan Upper Peninsula Pasties,
        155
    Pork and Duck Confit Pie, 139
    Post-Thanksgiving Turkey Pot Pie, *132*,
        133
    Roasted Curried Cauliflower
        Turnovers, 160, *161*
    Salmon Rolled Pie with Shrimp and
        Spinach Mousseline, 96, *97*
    Summer Tomato Tart, 120, *121*
tomatoes
    Beef Short Rib and Vegetable Pot Pie
        with Red Wine Sauce, *50*, 51–52
    Mediterranean Vegetable Pie, 88–90,
        91
    Summer Tomato Tart, 120, *121*
    Tomato, Basil, and Mozzarella Pie,
        130, *131*
tools and vessels, 20–23
turkey
    Post-Thanksgiving Turkey Pot Pie,
        132, 133

Turkey Stock, 133
turnovers
    about, 154
    Cornish-Style Pasties, *152*, 156–57
    Curried Chickpea Turnovers, 159
    Curried Duck or Chicken Turnovers,
        158
    Michigan Upper Peninsula Pasties,
        155
    Mom's Pierogis, 162, *163*
    Roasted Curried Cauliflower
        Turnovers, 160, *161*

V

vegetables. *See also specific vegetables*
    Beef Short Rib and Vegetable Pot Pie
        with Red Wine Sauce, *50*, 51–52
    Mediterranean Vegetable Pie, 88–90,
        91
    Pork Tenderloin with Root
        Vegetables and Mushrooms in
        Puff Pastry, 98, *201*
    Roasted Vegetable Pot Pie, 56
Venison Pot Pie, 64, *65*
vent hole, 27
Vol-au-Vent Pastry Shells, 168–69, *169*
vol-au-vents
    about, 166
    Crawfish and Andouille Vol-au-Vents,
        174, 175
    Creamed Morel and Asparagus Vol-
        au-Vents, 173
    Emincé of Chicken with Lemon,
        Tarragon, and Garlic Vol-au-
        Vents, *171*, 177
    Escargots with Parsley and Garlic
        Vol-au-Vents, 170, *171*
    making filling ahead for, 167
    Sautéed Gulf Shrimp with Cognac
        and Cream Vol-au-Vents, *171*, 172
    Seared Sea Scallop with Sweet Corn
        and Roasted Red Pepper Vol-au-
        Vents, 176

W

Walnut Crust, Stilton Cheesecake with,
    118, 119
water, 24
Watercress or Arugula, Roasted Beets
    with, 185
wine. *See also* sherry
    American Pekin Duck Pie with
        Pistachios, 134–37, *137*
    Beef Short Rib and Vegetable Pot
        Pie with Red Wine Sauce, *50*,
        51–52
    Red Currant Sauce, 193
    Spinach and Mushroom Galette, 116,
        117

Z

zucchini
    Mediterranean Vegetable Pie, 88–90,
        91

For information about permission to reproduce selections
from this book, write to Permissions, W. W. Norton &
Company, Inc., 500 Fifth Avenue, New York, NY 10110

For information about special discounts for bulk
purchases, please contact W. W. Norton Special Sales at
specialsales@wwnorton.com or 800-233-4830

Manufacturing by Transcontinental
Book design by Toni Tajima Design
Art director: Allison Chi
Production manager: Anna Oler

ISBN: 978-0-393-54171-7

W. W. Norton & Company, Inc.
500 Fifth Avenue, New York, N.Y. 10110
www.wwnorton.com

W. W. Norton & Company Ltd.
15 Carlisle Street, London W1D 3BS

1 2 3 4 5 6 7 8 9 0